THE CURIOUS EXPLORER

A CHILD'S GUIDE TO SCIENTIFIC DISCOVERY

DR. MINAKSHI BANSAL

DEDICATION

To my children, whose endless curiosity and boundless imagination inspire me every day. May this book ignite a spark of wonder in their hearts and set them on a lifelong journey of discovery. And to all the curious minds out there, young and old, who never cease to ask "why?" and "how?" May this book be your guide as you explore the wonders of science and unravel the mysteries of our world.

ƿƿƿ

Contents

Prayer   *ix*

About The Author   *xi*

Preface   *xv*

1. What Is Science? Asking Questions And Finding Cool   1
   Answers About The World.

Part 1

2. Why Do We Do Science? To Learn, Discover, And Make Life   7
   Better.

Part 2

3. What Is An Experiment? Like A Test, But For Finding Out   13
   How Things Work.

Part 3

4. What Is An Experiment? Like A Test, But For Finding Out   19
   How Things Work.

Part 4

5. What Are The Steps In Science? Ask, Guess, Test, Learn,   25
   Share!

Part 5

6. How Do Scientists Work Together? By Sharing Ideas And   31
   Building On Discoveries.

Part 6

7. What Tools Do Scientists Use? Everything From Telescopes   37
   To Tiny Tubes!

Part 7

8. What Is The Scientific Method? A Way To Ask And Answer   43
   Questions.

Contents

Part 8

   9. How Does Science Change? New Discoveries Lead To New   49
      Ideas.

Part 9

   10. Why Is Science Important? It Helps Us Understand And   55
      Improve Our World.

Part 10

   11. How Can I Be A Scientist? By Observing, Questioning, And   61
      Experimenting.

Part 11

   12. What Is Nature? The Incredible World Around Us, From   69
      Plants To Planets.

Part 12

   13. What Is Matter? The Stuff Everything Is Made Of.   75

Part 13

   14. What Is Energy? The Power That Makes Things Happen.   81

Part 14

   15. What Are The States Of Matter? Solid, Liquid, And Gas.   87

Part 15

   16. What Are The Different Types Of Energy? Light, Heat, Sound,   93
      And More!

Part 16

   17. What Are Atoms? The Tiny Building Blocks Of Everything.   99

Part 17

   18. How Do We Measure Things? Scientists Use Tools Like   105
      Rulers And Scales.

Contents

Part 18

19. What Are Scientific Theories? Big Ideas That Explain How   111
Things Work.

Part 19

20. What Are Scientific Laws? Rules That Describe How Nature   117
Behaves.

Part 20

21. How Does Science Help Us? It Leads To Inventions That   123
Improve Our Lives.

Part 21

22. Why Should We Protect Our Planet? To Keep It Healthy For   129
Us And All Living Things.

Part 22

23. How Can I Make A Difference? By Learning About Science   135
And Caring For Our World.

Part 23

24. SUMMARY   141

Part 24

Citation and References   147

Other Books of the Author   149

CONTACT   155

Prayer

"Om Bhadram Karnebhih Shrinuyama Devah

Bhadram Pashyemakshabhiryajatrah

Sthirairangais Tushtuvamsastanubhih

Vyashema Devahitam Yadayuh

Svasti Na Indro Vriddhashravah

Svasti Nah Pusha Vishwavedah

Svasti Nastarkshyo Arishtanemih

Svasti No Brihaspatir Dadhatu

Om Shantih Shantih Shantih"

This mantra is a prayer for universal well-being, invoking the blessings of various deities for protection, health, and happiness. It emphasizes the importance of experiencing the auspicious through all senses and living a life aligned with divine purpose. The repetition of "Shantih" at the end signifies a deep desire for peace in the individual, the environment, and the universe at large. This mantra is often recited as a prayer for peace, prosperity, and the physical and spiritual well-being of all beings.

ᐅᐅᐅ

About The Author

This book represents the culmination of extensive research and meticulous analysis, incorporating a diverse range of sources, including numerous books, scholarly studies, and personal experiences. Additionally, I have scoured various websites to gather relevant information and data essential for the compilation of this work. I have taken every precaution to ensure the accuracy of the information presented and have diligently cited all sources to acknowledge their contributions.

From her earliest days, Minakshi was distinguished by an insatiable appetite for reading. Her literary universe was inhabited by characters and narratives that spanned ethical tales, motivational and inspirational stories, and the mythic parables imbued with life lessons. This voracious reading habit was not merely for personal edification but was driven by a desire to distill and disseminate the essence of these narratives to foster the development of students and peers alike. She was particularly captivated by the lives and teachings of historical figures and spiritual leaders such as Adi Shankaracharya, Swami Vivekananda, Dr. APJ Abdul Kalam, Mahamana Pandit Madan Mohan Malviya, Mahatma Gandhi, Sardar Vallabhai Patel, and Vinoba Bhave, among others. Their philosophies and life stories fueled her ambition to embody their ideals of resilience, selflessness, and relentless pursuit of knowledge.

Dr. Minakshi's academic and practical engagement with psychology has been equally noteworthy. As a research scholar, her focus has been on exploring the intricate tapestry of the human psyche, aiming to unlock the potential for psychological well-being and societal harmony. Her scholarly work is complemented by her active involvement in social work, where she employs her academic insights to make tangible differences in the lives of the underprivileged. Her endeavours in social work are characterized by an innovative approach that combines traditional wisdom with contemporary psychological practices to address the multifaceted challenges faced by these communities.

Her artistic talents, another facet of her diverse capabilities, are not merely a personal passion but also serve as a medium through which she communicates and connects with others. Her art, rich in symbolism and emotional depth, reflects her philosophical inquiries and social concerns, offering viewers a glimpse into the breadth of her intellect and the depth of her compassion.

In addition to her contributions to the arts and social sciences, Dr. Minakshi has embraced the healing arts of Pranic Healing, mastering the techniques developed by Master Choa Kok Sui. This practice, which focuses on the manipulation of Prana or life energy to heal the body and aura, has been both a personal journey of discovery and a means through which she extends her healing touch to others. Her proficiency in Pranic Healing is complemented by her advocacy and teaching of various forms of meditation aimed at rejuvenation, personal betterment, and the cultivation of harmony within individuals and communities alike.

Dr. Minakshi's life is a narrative of relentless pursuit, not just of personal achievement but of the upliftment and empowerment of society at large. Her diverse interests and talents—spanning the arts, literature, psychology, and the healing practices—converge on a singular path of service. She embodies the spirit of the luminaries who inspired her, channelling their legacy through her actions and teachings. Through her books, art, and social initiatives, she continues to inspire a new generation to embark on their own journeys of self-discovery, resilience, and altruism.

Her commitment to social betterment, particularly her focus on uplifting underprivileged children, reflects a deep understanding of the transformative potential of education and personal development. By integrating her knowledge of psychology, her artistic sensibilities, and her healing practices, Dr. Bansal has developed a holistic approach to social work that addresses both the immediate needs and the long-term well-being of the communities she serves.

As an author, Dr. Minakshi's writings offer a blend of inspirational insights, practical wisdom, and reflective contemplations drawn from her extensive reading and life experiences. Her books serve as a guide for those seeking to navigate the complexities of life with grace, resilience, and purpose. Through her narratives, she extends an invitation to her readers to explore the depths of their own potential and to contribute meaningfully to the collective well-being of society.

In Dr. Minakshi Bansal, we find a remarkable synthesis of the artist, the scholar, the healer, and the social activist. Her life's work stands as a beacon of hope and a source of inspiration for individuals seeking to make a difference in the world. Her story is a compelling reminder of the power of individual action, rooted in compassion and driven by a profound commitment to the betterment of humanity. Dr. Minakshi's legacy is not just in the tangible outcomes of her efforts but in the enduring spirit of inquiry, empathy, and service that she embodies.

Preface

In a world brimming with wonders, children possess a natural curiosity that sparks a lifelong quest for knowledge. As a mother, educator, and scientist, I've always been fascinated by the way children's eyes light up with questions about the world around them. Why is the sky blue? How do birds fly? Where does the sun go at night? These simple questions often lead to profound discoveries, and it is in this spirit of curiosity and exploration that I embarked on the creation of this book.

In this book, I invite young readers to embark on an exciting journey into the world of science. My aim is to ignite their imaginations, spark their curiosity, and nurture a lifelong love of learning. Science is not just a subject to be studied in school; it is a way of understanding the world, a framework for asking questions, and a powerful tool for solving problems and making informed decisions.

This book is not a comprehensive encyclopedia of scientific facts; rather, it is a playful and engaging introduction to the fundamental concepts of science. It encourages children to observe the world around them, to ask questions, and to seek answers through experimentation and exploration. It celebrates the joy of discovery and the thrill of understanding how things work.

Throughout this book, I have tried to make science accessible and fun for young readers. I have used simple language, vivid illustrations, and hands-on activities to bring scientific concepts to life. I have also included stories of real scientists and their discoveries, highlighting the diversity of backgrounds and perspectives that contribute to the scientific enterprise.

This book covers a wide range of scientific topics, from the basic building blocks of matter to the vastness of the cosmos. It explores the wonders of nature, from the smallest insects to the largest mammals, and delves into the mysteries of the human body. It also examines the impact of science on our daily lives, from the food we eat to the technology we use.

Each chapter in this book is designed to be a self-contained exploration of a particular scientific topic. However, the chapters are also interconnected, building upon each other to create a comprehensive picture of the world of science. The book also includes a glossary of scientific terms, a list of resources for further exploration, and suggestions for hands-on activities that children can do at home or in the classroom.

I have written this book with the help of artificial intelligence, a powerful tool that has the potential to revolutionize education. AI has allowed me to access and analyze vast amounts of information, to personalize learning experiences for individual readers, and to create interactive activities that engage and motivate young learners.

However, I want to emphasize that AI is not a replacement for human creativity and expertise. It is a tool, not a substitute. The heart and soul of this book come from my own passion for science and my desire to share that passion with children. AI has simply helped me to express that passion in a more engaging and effective way.

My hope is that this book will inspire a new generation of scientists, engineers, and innovators. But more importantly, I hope it will inspire a generation of critical thinkers, problem solvers, and lifelong learners. Science is not just about facts and figures; it is about asking questions, seeking answers, and exploring the world around us with wonder and curiosity.

I encourage you to read this book with your children, to share their excitement as they discover new things, and to support their curiosity as they embark on their own scientific adventures. Remember, every child is a scientist at heart, eager to explore the world and uncover its secrets. It is our responsibility as adults to nurture that curiosity and provide them with the tools and opportunities they need to thrive.

Let us together embark on this journey of discovery, where science is not just a subject but a way of life, a lens through which we view the world and a source of endless fascination and inspiration.

Dr. Minakshi Bansal
Social Activist
Ahmedabad, Gujarat, Bharat

ONE

WHAT IS SCIENCE? ASKING QUESTIONS AND FINDING COOL ANSWERS ABOUT THE WORLD.

Have you ever looked up at the night sky and wondered what those twinkling lights are? Or maybe you've watched a tiny seed grow into a towering sunflower and thought, "How does that happen?" If so, you've already taken the first step on the amazing journey of science! Science isn't just about facts and figures in textbooks; it's about the thrill of asking questions and the joy of finding out how the world works.

Imagine yourself as a detective, but instead of solving crimes, you're solving mysteries about the universe. Science is your magnifying glass, helping you examine the smallest details and the grandest pictures. Why does the sky change color at sunset? Why does a ball bounce? How do birds know where to fly for winter? These are the kinds of questions scientists ask, and the answers are often surprising and exciting.

When we say science is about asking questions, we don't mean just any old question. "What's your favorite ice cream flavor?" is fun to ask, but it doesn't help us learn about the world. Scientific questions are special because they are testable. That means we can try things out, experiment, and gather evidence to see if our guesses are right.

Scientists use a special method, a bit like a recipe, to tackle these questions. First, they carefully observe something interesting. Maybe they notice bees buzzing around a flower, or a strange rock formation in a canyon. Then, they come up with an idea or "hypothesis" about why this is happening. It's like making a guess, but a smart guess based on what they already know.

Next, they design an experiment to test their hypothesis. This is the fun part! It might involve mixing chemicals in a lab, watching animals in their natural habitat, or even launching a rocket into space. By gathering data and making observations, scientists can see if their guess holds up or if they need to rethink things.

What happens if the experiment doesn't support their hypothesis? That's okay! In science, even "wrong" answers are valuable because they teach us something new. Scientists learn from their mistakes and come up with new and better ideas. This constant cycle of questioning, experimenting, and learning is what makes science so dynamic and exciting.

But science isn't just about being curious; it's also about finding cool answers. Have you ever heard of dinosaurs, those giant creatures that roamed the Earth millions of years ago? We know about them because scientists have carefully studied fossils, which are like clues from the past. They've used this evidence to piece together amazing stories about what life was like back then.

Or consider how we understand outer space. Telescopes are like giant eyes that let us see faraway planets and galaxies. Scientists have used these tools to discover new worlds, learn about black holes, and even find evidence that there might be other life forms out there in the universe!

Science isn't just for grown-ups in lab coats, either. Everyone can be a scientist, no matter how old you are. Just by looking around, asking questions, and trying things out, you're already doing science. Have you ever built a sandcastle and wondered why it sticks together? Or made a paper airplane and tried to figure out how to make it fly farther? These are experiments!

You can even do science in your kitchen. Why not try mixing different ingredients to see how they react? Or experiment with making slime or homemade ice cream? The possibilities are endless, and the more you explore, the more you'll discover the wonders of the world around you.

So, the next time you see something interesting, don't just say, "Wow!" Ask "Why?" Be curious, ask questions, and let science be your guide as you embark on the greatest adventure of all: the adventure of understanding the universe!

ᐅᐅᐅ

"Curiosity is the spark that ignites the flame of discovery. Ask questions, seek answers, and never stop exploring the wonders of the world around you."

TWO

WHY DO WE DO SCIENCE? TO LEARN, DISCOVER, AND MAKE LIFE BETTER.

From the moment we open our eyes as infants, we embark on a lifelong journey of learning and discovery. We reach out to touch, taste, and explore the world around us, driven by an innate curiosity. This insatiable thirst for knowledge is at the heart of why we do science. Science is not merely a collection of facts; it's a dynamic process that fuels our understanding of the universe and empowers us to improve our lives in countless ways.

Learning is the foundation of science. Every scientific endeavor begins with a question, a spark of curiosity that ignites the pursuit of knowledge. Why does the sun rise and set? What are the stars made of? How do plants grow? These questions and countless others have driven humans to explore, experiment, and uncover the secrets of nature. Through careful observation, meticulous experimentation, and rigorous analysis, scientists have pieced together a vast tapestry of knowledge that illuminates the workings of the world around us.

But science is not just about accumulating facts; it's about discovering the underlying principles that govern the universe. When Isaac Newton observed an apple falling from a tree, he didn't just see a piece of fruit dropping to the ground; he saw a universal force at play—gravity. This single discovery revolutionized our understanding of the cosmos and laid the groundwork for countless technological advancements. From the laws of motion to the theory of relativity, scientific discoveries have unveiled the fundamental principles that shape our reality.

The pursuit of knowledge through science has not only expanded our understanding of the natural world but has also transformed our lives in profound ways. Scientific discoveries have led to groundbreaking innovations that have improved our health, enriched our lives, and reshaped our society. Vaccines have eradicated deadly diseases, antibiotics have saved countless lives, and medical imaging technologies have revolutionized healthcare.

Science has also empowered us to harness the forces of nature for our benefit. Electricity, powered by scientific understanding of electromagnetism, has illuminated our homes, fueled our industries, and connected us across vast distances. The development of agriculture, driven by scientific research into plant breeding and crop management, has enabled us to feed a growing global population. Transportation technologies, from the steam engine to the airplane, have shrunk the world and opened up new horizons for exploration and trade.

Beyond its practical applications, science has enriched our lives in countless ways. The study of astronomy has revealed the vastness and beauty of the cosmos, inspiring awe and wonder. The exploration of the human genome has unlocked the secrets of our genetic heritage, shedding light on our origins and potential. The study of history has revealed the rich tapestry of human experience, providing valuable lessons for the present and future.

But perhaps the most compelling reason why we do science is the hope of creating a better future for ourselves and generations to come. Climate change, disease, poverty, and inequality are just a few of the global challenges that science can help us address. By developing clean energy technologies, finding cures for diseases, and promoting sustainable practices, science has the potential to create a more just, equitable, and sustainable world.

Of course, science is not without its challenges. The pursuit of knowledge can be fraught with setbacks, controversies, and ethical dilemmas. Scientific discoveries can raise questions about the nature of life, the limits of technology, and the responsibilities that come with knowledge. But these challenges are also opportunities for growth and reflection. By engaging in open and honest dialogue, by upholding ethical principles, and by prioritizing the well-being of humanity and the planet, we can ensure that science remains a force for good in the world.

In the end, science is not just about what we know; it's about who we are. It's a testament to our insatiable curiosity, our relentless pursuit of knowledge, and our unwavering belief in the power of human ingenuity. By embracing science, we embrace our potential to create a brighter future for ourselves and for generations to come. So let us continue to ask questions, to explore, to discover, and to use the power of science to make life better for all.

"Science isn't just about facts in textbooks; it's about the thrill of asking 'why?' and the joy of figuring out how things work. So, be a detective of the universe and let your curiosity lead the way!"

THREE

WHAT IS AN EXPERIMENT? LIKE A TEST, BUT FOR FINDING OUT HOW THINGS WORK.

Have you ever wondered why a balloon floats or how a magnet attracts metal? Or perhaps you've pondered why plants need sunlight to grow? These questions, big and small, have sparked curiosity in humans for centuries. And to answer them, we turn to a powerful tool: the experiment.

An experiment is like a playful test, a carefully designed activity that allows us to investigate the world around us. It's a way of asking nature a question and seeing how it responds. Just as a detective gathers clues to solve a mystery, a scientist gathers data through experiments to uncover the hidden workings of the universe.

Imagine you have a box filled with colorful blocks of different shapes and sizes. You might wonder: which blocks are the heaviest? Which ones float in water? Which ones make the loudest sound when dropped? To answer these questions, you could simply guess, but that wouldn't be very reliable. Instead, you could conduct experiments. You could weigh each block on a scale, drop them in a tub of water, or listen to the sounds they make when they hit the floor. By carefully observing and recording your results, you would be well on your way to answering your questions.

In a similar way, scientists use experiments to test their ideas about how the world works. These ideas, called hypotheses, are like educated guesses based on observations and prior knowledge. A hypothesis might suggest that a certain type of fertilizer makes plants grow faster, or that a particular gene is responsible for a specific trait in an animal. To test these hypotheses, scientists design experiments that carefully control the variables involved.

A variable is any factor that can change in an experiment. For example, in a plant growth experiment, variables might include the amount of sunlight, water, and fertilizer each plant receives. The scientist would manipulate one variable at a time, keeping all other variables constant, to see how it affects the plants' growth. By comparing the results of different treatments, the scientist can determine whether their hypothesis is supported or not.

Experiments are not always conducted in a laboratory with fancy equipment. They can be as simple as observing the behavior of animals in their natural habitat or testing the effectiveness of a new recipe in your kitchen. The key is to have a clear question, a testable hypothesis, and a well-designed plan for collecting data.

The process of experimentation is often iterative, meaning that scientists repeat their experiments multiple times to ensure their results are reliable. They also share their findings with other scientists, who can then replicate the experiments and verify the results. This collaborative process helps to build a solid foundation of scientific knowledge.

Experiments are not always straightforward, and unexpected results can sometimes lead to even more exciting discoveries. For example, Alexander Fleming, a Scottish scientist, accidentally discovered penicillin, the first antibiotic, when he noticed that a mold growing on a petri dish was inhibiting the growth of bacteria. This serendipitous discovery revolutionized medicine and saved countless lives.

In addition to testing hypotheses, experiments can also be used to explore new phenomena and develop new technologies. For example, experiments with electricity led to the invention of the light bulb, the telephone, and the computer. Experiments with materials have led to the development of new fabrics, building materials, and medical implants.

The power of experimentation lies not only in its ability to answer questions but also in its ability to spark new questions and inspire further inquiry. Each experiment is a stepping stone on the path to greater understanding. As we continue to experiment, we unlock the secrets of the universe and pave the way for a brighter future.

But experiments are not just for scientists. They are for anyone with a curious mind and a willingness to explore. By conducting simple experiments at home or in the classroom, children can develop a love of science and a deeper appreciation for the world around them. They can learn to think critically, solve problems, and appreciate the importance of evidence-based reasoning.

So, the next time you encounter a mystery or have a question about how something works, don't be afraid to experiment. Ask questions, make observations, and test your ideas. You might be surprised at what you discover. Remember, the world is a vast and wondrous laboratory, and the possibilities for exploration are endless.

◁◁◁

"Think of an experiment like a playful test. You get to ask nature a question and see what it says back! It's like having a conversation with the world itself."

FOUR

WHAT IS AN EXPERIMENT? LIKE A TEST, BUT FOR FINDING OUT HOW THINGS WORK.

Imagine you're on a treasure hunt. You have a map with clues, but you don't know exactly where the treasure is hidden. What do you do? You start by asking questions: "Where should I start looking? What kind of terrain am I dealing with? Are there any landmarks to guide me?" Then, you make a guess, or hypothesis, about where the treasure might be. You test your guess by following the map and looking for clues. As you explore, you learn more about the area and refine your search. Finally, when you find the treasure, you share your discovery with others.

This is the essence of the scientific method, the series of steps that scientists follow to explore the world around us. While it may seem complex at first, the core idea is simple: ask questions, make guesses, test those guesses, learn from the results, and share your findings with others. Let's take a closer look at each step of this exciting adventure.

Asking: The Spark of Curiosity

Every scientific journey begins with a question. It could be a simple question, like "Why is the sky blue?" or a more complex one, like "How do vaccines work?" These questions stem from our innate curiosity, our desire to understand the world around us. They are the spark that ignites the scientific process.

When asking questions, scientists try to be as specific and focused as possible. They also try to frame their questions in a way that can be tested through experimentation or observation. For example, instead of asking "Why is the sky blue?", a scientist might ask "What causes the sky to appear blue?" This allows them to focus their investigation and design experiments that can help them find answers.

Guessing: The Hypothesis

Once a scientist has a question, they make an educated guess, or hypothesis, about the answer. This is based on their existing knowledge, observations, and any relevant scientific theories. A hypothesis is not just a random guess; it's a testable explanation for a phenomenon. It's like a possible solution to a puzzle, waiting to be confirmed or refuted.

For example, if a scientist is investigating why some plants grow taller than others, they might hypothesize that the amount of sunlight a plant receives affects its growth. This hypothesis can be tested by conducting experiments in which different groups of plants are exposed to varying amounts of sunlight.

Testing: The Experiment

The next step is to design and conduct experiments to test the hypothesis. This involves carefully controlling the variables involved and collecting data through observation and measurement. The goal is to see if the results of the experiment support or contradict the hypothesis.

In our plant growth experiment, the scientist might set up several groups of plants, each receiving a different amount of sunlight. They would then measure the height of the plants over time and compare the results. If the plants receiving more sunlight consistently grow taller, this would support the hypothesis. However, if there is no clear difference in growth, or if the plants receiving less sunlight grow taller, this would cast doubt on the hypothesis.

Learning: Analyzing the Results

After conducting an experiment, scientists carefully analyze the data they have collected. They look for patterns, trends, and relationships between variables. They also consider any potential sources of error or bias in their experiment.

The analysis of data can be complex, involving statistical tests and mathematical models. The goal is to draw meaningful conclusions from the data and determine whether the hypothesis is supported or not. If the hypothesis is supported, this adds to our scientific knowledge and helps us understand the world better. If the hypothesis is not supported, this can also be valuable, as it can lead to new questions and new avenues of research.

Sharing: Communicating the Findings

The final step in the scientific process is to share the findings with others. This can be done through scientific publications, presentations at conferences, or educational outreach programs. By sharing their results, scientists contribute to the collective body of scientific knowledge and allow others to build upon their work.

Sharing results also allows for peer review, a process in which other scientists evaluate the quality and validity of the research. This helps to ensure that scientific findings are reliable and robust. It also allows for the identification of potential flaws in the experiment or alternative interpretations of the data.

The scientific method is not a rigid set of rules, but rather a flexible framework that can be adapted to different types of investigations. It's a powerful tool for exploring the world around us, but it's important to remember that it's not infallible. Scientific knowledge is constantly evolving as new evidence emerges and old ideas are challenged.

By embracing the process of asking, guessing, testing, learning, and sharing, we can all participate in the exciting adventure of scientific discovery. Whether you're a professional scientist or a curious child, the scientific method offers a path to understanding the world and making meaningful contributions to our collective knowledge.

ϷϷϷ

"Scientists aren't just people in lab coats. They're explorers, inventors, and even kids like you! Anyone who's curious about the world can be a scientist."

FIVE

WHAT ARE THE STEPS IN SCIENCE? ASK, GUESS, TEST, LEARN, SHARE!

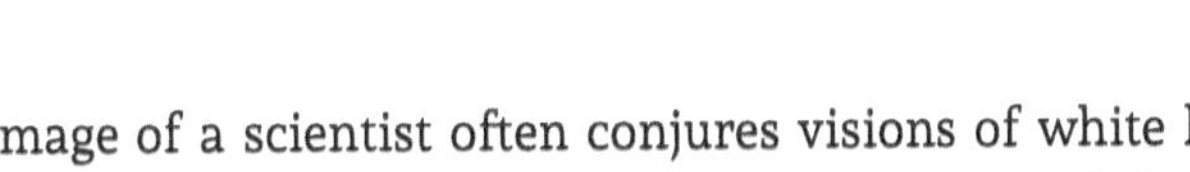

The image of a scientist often conjures visions of white lab coats, bubbling beakers, and complex equations scrawled across a chalkboard. While these are certainly aspects of scientific work, the true essence of a scientist lies in something far more fundamental: curiosity.

At their core, scientists are individuals who possess an insatiable thirst for knowledge and a deep-seated desire to understand the world around them. They are driven by a relentless curiosity that propels them to ask questions, seek answers, and uncover the hidden mysteries of the universe.

Scientists come from all walks of life and hail from diverse backgrounds. They may be young or old, male or female, from any cultural or ethnic group. What unites them is their shared passion for exploration and discovery. They are the explorers of our time, venturing into the unknown realms of nature, unraveling the secrets of the cosmos, and pushing the boundaries of human knowledge.

Curiosity is the driving force behind every scientific endeavor. It is the spark that ignites the quest for knowledge, the fuel that propels scientists to ask "why?" and "how?" It is the insatiable thirst that compels them to seek answers, to delve deeper into the mysteries of the universe, and to unravel the complex tapestry of nature.

The curious mind of a scientist is never content with the status quo. It constantly seeks new challenges, new frontiers to conquer. It questions assumptions, challenges conventional wisdom, and dares to think outside the box. It is a mind that is constantly learning, growing, and evolving.

Scientists are not afraid to ask seemingly simple questions, for they know that even the most basic inquiries can lead to profound discoveries. They understand that the path to knowledge is often paved with seemingly trivial observations and unexpected connections.

Curiosity is not just about asking questions; it is also about seeking answers. Scientists are relentless in their pursuit of knowledge, employing a wide range of tools and techniques to investigate the world around them. They design experiments, collect data, analyze results, and draw conclusions. They build models, develop theories, and test hypotheses.

The quest for answers is not always easy. It can be frustrating, time-consuming, and even discouraging at times. But for scientists, the thrill of discovery is worth the effort. The "aha!" moment, when a new piece of the puzzle falls into place, is a reward that fuels their passion and drives them to continue their explorations.

Scientists are not solitary figures working in isolation. They are part of a vibrant community of like-minded individuals who share their passion for knowledge. They collaborate, exchange ideas, and build upon each other's work. They attend conferences, publish papers, and engage in lively debates.

This collaborative spirit is essential to the advancement of science. By sharing their findings and ideas, scientists accelerate the pace of discovery and ensure that their work has a broader impact. They also benefit from the insights and expertise of others, which can help them refine their own research and overcome challenges.

Scientists are not just researchers; they are also communicators. They have a responsibility to share their findings with the public and to explain complex scientific concepts in ways that are accessible and engaging. They write books, articles, and blog posts. They give talks, lectures, and interviews. They use social media to connect with a wider audience.

By communicating their work effectively, scientists inspire others to explore the wonders of science and to appreciate the importance of evidence-based reasoning. They also help to build public trust in science and to ensure that scientific knowledge is used for the benefit of society.

The curiosity of scientists is not limited to their professional lives. It extends to all aspects of their existence. They are lifelong learners, constantly seeking new knowledge and experiences. They are avid readers, travelers, and explorers. They are fascinated by art, music, and literature.

This wide range of interests enriches their lives and informs their work. It allows them to see the world from different perspectives and to make connections between seemingly disparate fields. It also helps them to communicate their work to a wider audience and to inspire others to embrace the spirit of inquiry.

So, what is a scientist? A scientist is anyone who is curious about the world. It is someone who asks questions, seeks answers, and shares their findings with others. It is someone who is driven by a passion for exploration and discovery. It is someone who is constantly learning, growing, and evolving.

Whether you are a professional scientist or simply someone who is curious about the world, embrace your curiosity. Ask questions, seek answers, and never stop learning. The world is full of wonders waiting to be discovered.

ᕹᕹᕹ

"Working together is the key to scientific success.
Just like a team builds a tower, scientists build on
each other's ideas to make amazing discoveries."

SIX

How do scientists work together? By sharing ideas and building on discoveries.

The image of a lone scientist toiling away in a secluded laboratory, Eureka moment striking like a lightning bolt, is a captivating one. Yet, the reality of scientific progress is far more collaborative and interconnected. Science thrives on the exchange of ideas, the building upon previous discoveries, and the collective efforts of countless individuals working together towards a common goal. It is a symphony of collaboration, where the harmonious interplay of diverse minds leads to breakthroughs that would be impossible for any one person to achieve alone.

At its core, science is a social endeavor. Scientists are not isolated figures working in silos; they are part of a vast network of researchers, scholars, and practitioners who share a common passion for understanding the world around us. This network spans continents, cultures, and disciplines, connecting individuals who may never meet face-to-face but whose work is inextricably linked.

The exchange of ideas is the lifeblood of scientific progress. Scientists communicate their findings through a variety of channels, including peer-reviewed journals, conferences, seminars, and online platforms. This open exchange allows for critical feedback, validation of results, and the identification of potential flaws or limitations in research. It also sparks new ideas, as scientists build upon each other's work, challenge existing assumptions, and explore new avenues of inquiry.

Scientific conferences and workshops are particularly vibrant hubs of collaboration. These gatherings bring together researchers from diverse backgrounds and disciplines, creating a fertile ground for cross-pollination of ideas. Scientists present their latest findings, engage in lively discussions, and forge new collaborations. The energy and enthusiasm at these events are palpable, as scientists share their passion for discovery and inspire each other to reach new heights.

The sharing of data and resources is another critical aspect of scientific collaboration. In many fields, large-scale projects require the combined efforts of numerous researchers and institutions. For example, the Human Genome Project, which sequenced the entire human genome, involved the collaboration of thousands of scientists from around the world. Similarly, the Large Hadron Collider, the world's largest and most powerful particle accelerator, is a collaborative effort involving scientists from over 100 countries.

By pooling their resources and expertise, scientists can tackle complex problems that would be insurmountable for any individual or single institution. They can also share the costs and risks associated with large-scale projects, making it possible to pursue ambitious research goals that would otherwise be out of reach.

Mentorship and training are also vital components of scientific collaboration. Senior scientists play a crucial role in guiding and nurturing the next generation of researchers. They share their knowledge, experience, and insights, helping young scientists develop the skills and expertise they need to succeed. They also provide opportunities for collaboration and networking, opening doors for young scientists to contribute to cutting-edge research and make their mark on the field.

Scientific collaboration is not always smooth sailing. Differences in opinions, approaches, and priorities can lead to conflicts and disagreements. However, these challenges can also be opportunities for growth and learning. By engaging in open and respectful dialogue, scientists can find common ground, resolve conflicts, and forge stronger collaborations.

The advent of digital technologies has revolutionized scientific collaboration. Online platforms and tools have made it easier than ever for scientists to connect with each other, share data, and collaborate on projects regardless of their geographical location. Virtual conferences, webinars, and online forums have broken down barriers and fostered a more inclusive and global scientific community.

Social media has also played a role in facilitating scientific collaboration. Platforms like Twitter and ResearchGate allow scientists to share their work, connect with colleagues, and engage in real-time discussions. These platforms have also helped to democratize science, giving a voice to researchers from underrepresented groups and fostering a more diverse and inclusive scientific community.

The benefits of scientific collaboration are undeniable. By working together, scientists can achieve more than they ever could alone. They can tackle complex problems, accelerate the pace of discovery, and translate their findings into real-world solutions that benefit society. Collaboration also fosters a sense of community and shared purpose, creating a supportive environment where scientists can thrive.

In today's rapidly changing world, scientific collaboration is more important than ever. The challenges we face, from climate change to pandemics to social inequality, require a concerted effort from scientists across disciplines and borders. By embracing collaboration and building upon each other's discoveries, we can harness the power of science to create a brighter future for all.

ppp

"Scientists use tools like telescopes to see faraway stars and microscopes to see tiny creatures. They're like superpowers that help us understand the big and small wonders of the universe."

SEVEN

WHAT TOOLS DO SCIENTISTS USE? EVERYTHING FROM TELESCOPES TO TINY TUBES!

Imagine a toolbox overflowing with gadgets, instruments, and contraptions of all shapes and sizes. This is the world of scientific tools, a vast and ever-expanding collection of instruments that empower scientists to explore the universe, from the vast expanse of the cosmos to the intricate workings of a single cell.

From the earliest days of human inquiry, scientists have relied on tools to extend their senses and probe the mysteries of nature. Galileo Galilei, the Italian astronomer, used a simple telescope to observe the moons of Jupiter, shattering the prevailing view of a geocentric universe. Antonie van Leeuwenhoek, the Dutch microscopist, crafted his own lenses to peer into a hidden world of microorganisms, revealing a teeming universe of life invisible to the naked eye.

Today, scientists have at their disposal an astonishing array of tools that would have seemed like science fiction to their predecessors. These tools range from the familiar, such as microscopes and telescopes, to the cutting-edge, such as particle accelerators and gene sequencers. Each tool is designed to answer a specific question, to measure a particular phenomenon, or to manipulate matter in a precise way.

At the largest scale, telescopes are the eyes of astronomers, allowing them to peer into the depths of space and observe distant stars, galaxies, and nebulae. Telescopes come in many varieties, from optical telescopes that collect visible light to radio telescopes that detect radio waves emitted by celestial objects. Some telescopes are even launched into space, where they can observe the universe without the interference of Earth's atmosphere.

On Earth, geologists use a variety of tools to study the planet's structure and composition. Seismographs measure the vibrations of earthquakes, providing clues about the Earth's interior. Rock hammers and hand lenses are used to examine rocks and minerals in the field, while more sophisticated instruments, such as X-ray diffractometers, are used to analyze the chemical composition of geological samples.

In the life sciences, microscopes are essential tools for biologists and medical researchers. These instruments allow scientists to magnify tiny objects, such as cells, bacteria, and viruses, revealing their intricate structures and functions. Electron microscopes, which use beams of electrons instead of light, can magnify objects millions of times, allowing scientists to visualize even the smallest molecules.

Chemists use a wide range of tools to analyze and manipulate matter. Spectrometers measure the absorption or emission of light by different substances, providing information about their chemical composition. Chromatographs separate mixtures into their individual components, while mass spectrometers identify and quantify the molecules present in a sample.

In recent decades, the development of powerful computers and sophisticated software has revolutionized scientific research. Computers are used to collect, store, and analyze vast amounts of data, allowing scientists to identify patterns, trends, and correlations that would be impossible to detect manually. They are also used to model complex systems, such as the Earth's climate or the human brain, and to simulate experiments that would be too dangerous or expensive to conduct in the real world.

The tools of science are not limited to physical instruments. Scientists also rely on a variety of conceptual tools, such as mathematical models, statistical methods, and computer simulations. These tools allow scientists to represent complex phenomena in a simplified form, making them easier to understand and analyze. They also enable scientists to make predictions about future events and to test the validity of their hypotheses.

The development of new scientific tools is an ongoing process, driven by the ever-expanding frontiers of knowledge. As scientists delve deeper into the mysteries of nature, they encounter new challenges that require new tools to overcome. For example, the study of nanotechnology, which deals with materials and devices at the atomic and molecular scale, has required the development of entirely new types of microscopes and manipulators.

The impact of scientific tools on society has been profound. They have revolutionized our understanding of the universe, transformed our lives, and opened up new possibilities for the future. From the development of life-saving vaccines to the exploration of outer space, scientific tools have played a crucial role in shaping our world.

The use of scientific tools is not without its challenges. Some tools, such as particle accelerators and gene sequencers, are incredibly complex and expensive, requiring specialized training and infrastructure. The interpretation of data generated by these tools can also be challenging, as scientists must carefully consider potential sources of error and bias.

Ethical considerations also come into play when using scientific tools. For example, the development of powerful gene editing technologies raises questions about the potential risks and benefits of altering the human genome. Scientists must grapple with these ethical dilemmas and ensure that their work is conducted responsibly and for the betterment of society.

Despite these challenges, the power of scientific tools is undeniable. They are the keys that unlock the secrets of nature, the instruments that allow us to explore the universe and understand our place within it. As we continue to develop new and more sophisticated tools, the possibilities for discovery are limitless.

The next time you look up at the stars or marvel at the intricate workings of a flower, remember that behind every scientific discovery is a tool, a testament to human ingenuity and our insatiable thirst for knowledge. From telescopes to tiny tubes, these tools are the instruments of our curiosity, the keys that unlock the doors to a deeper understanding of the world around us.

ppp

"The scientific method is like a treasure map. It helps us ask the right questions, find the best clues, and ultimately uncover the truth about how things work."

EIGHT

WHAT IS THE SCIENTIFIC METHOD? A WAY TO ASK AND ANSWER QUESTIONS.

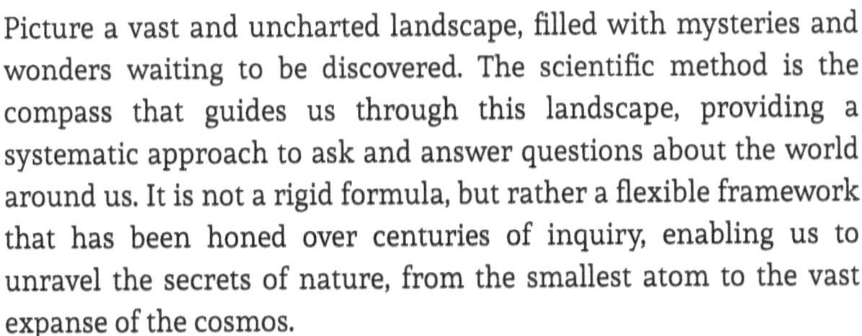

Picture a vast and uncharted landscape, filled with mysteries and wonders waiting to be discovered. The scientific method is the compass that guides us through this landscape, providing a systematic approach to ask and answer questions about the world around us. It is not a rigid formula, but rather a flexible framework that has been honed over centuries of inquiry, enabling us to unravel the secrets of nature, from the smallest atom to the vast expanse of the cosmos.

At its heart, the scientific method is a process of inquiry, a way of approaching questions with a skeptical mind and a thirst for evidence-based answers. It is not about dogma or blind faith; it is about seeking truth through rigorous observation, experimentation, and analysis. It is a journey of discovery, where each step brings us closer to understanding the underlying principles that govern the universe.

The scientific method typically begins with observation. We notice something interesting or puzzling in the world around us, sparking our curiosity and prompting us to ask questions. Why does the sun rise and set? Why do some animals hibernate? What causes disease? These questions are the starting point of our scientific inquiry.

Once we have a question, we formulate a hypothesis, a tentative explanation for the phenomenon we are observing. A hypothesis is not just a wild guess; it is an educated guess based on existing knowledge and observations. It is a testable statement that can be either supported or refuted by evidence.

To test our hypothesis, we design and conduct experiments. An experiment is a carefully controlled procedure designed to isolate and manipulate variables in order to observe their effects. By systematically changing one variable at a time and observing the results, we can determine whether our hypothesis is supported or not.

Experiments are not always possible or practical. In some cases, scientists rely on observation and data collection to test their hypotheses. For example, astronomers cannot conduct experiments on distant stars, but they can observe them through telescopes and collect data about their brightness, temperature, and composition. This data can then be used to test hypotheses about the formation and evolution of stars.

The analysis of data is a crucial step in the scientific method. Scientists use a variety of tools and techniques to analyze their data, including statistical analysis, mathematical modeling, and computer simulations. The goal is to identify patterns, trends, and relationships in the data that can help to confirm or refute the hypothesis.

If the data supports the hypothesis, this strengthens our confidence in the explanation and may lead to further investigations. If the data does not support the hypothesis, this does not necessarily mean that the hypothesis is wrong. It may simply mean that the experiment was flawed or that there are other factors at play that were not taken into account. In this case, scientists may revise their hypothesis or design new experiments to gather more evidence.

The scientific method is not a linear process; it is an iterative one. Scientists may go back and forth between different steps, refining their questions, revising their hypotheses, and designing new experiments as they gather more information. This continuous cycle of inquiry is what drives scientific progress.

The communication of findings is an essential part of the scientific method. Scientists share their results with other scientists through publications, presentations, and conferences. This allows other scientists to scrutinize their work, replicate their experiments, and build upon their findings. It also allows for the identification of errors or biases in the research and ensures that scientific knowledge is constantly being refined and improved.

The scientific method is not just a tool for scientists; it is a way of thinking that can be applied to many aspects of life. By approaching problems with a skeptical mind, seeking evidence-based answers, and being open to revising our beliefs in light of new information, we can make better decisions and avoid falling prey to misinformation and pseudoscience.

The scientific method is not perfect. It is limited by our current knowledge and technology, and it is subject to human error and bias. However, it is the best tool we have for understanding the world around us. By embracing the scientific method, we embrace a spirit of inquiry and a commitment to evidence-based reasoning. We open ourselves up to the possibility of new discoveries, new understandings, and new ways of seeing the world.

The scientific method is a powerful tool that has revolutionized our understanding of the universe and our place within it. It has led to countless breakthroughs in medicine, technology, and our understanding of the natural world. It is a testament to human curiosity and our relentless pursuit of knowledge. By embracing the scientific method, we continue the legacy of generations of scientists who have sought to understand the world around us, and we pave the way for future discoveries that will shape the course of human history.

ppp

"New discoveries are like stepping stones that lead to even more exciting ideas. Science is a journey that's always changing, and you get to be a part of it!"

NINE

How does science change? New discoveries lead to new ideas.

The world of science is not a stagnant pond but a rushing river, constantly evolving and adapting as new discoveries shape its course. This dynamic nature is one of the most exciting aspects of science, as it challenges us to constantly re-evaluate our understanding of the universe and our place within it. New discoveries are the lifeblood of scientific progress, pushing the boundaries of knowledge and inspiring new ideas that transform our world.

Imagine a world where the sun revolved around the Earth, where diseases were thought to be caused by imbalances in the body's humors, and where the atom was considered the smallest indivisible unit of matter. These were once widely accepted scientific beliefs, but they have all been overturned by new discoveries that challenged the prevailing paradigms of their time.

The history of science is replete with examples of how new discoveries have revolutionized our understanding of the world. The discovery of the double helix structure of DNA in 1953 by James Watson and Francis Crick ushered in a new era of genetic research, leading to breakthroughs in medicine, agriculture, and biotechnology. The discovery of the cosmic microwave background radiation in 1964 provided compelling evidence for the Big Bang theory, transforming our understanding of the origins of the universe.

New discoveries not only challenge existing ideas but also inspire new ones. When scientists uncover a new piece of the puzzle, it often opens up a whole new realm of possibilities. For example, the discovery of penicillin, the first antibiotic, in 1928 by Alexander Fleming led to a revolution in medicine, paving the way for the development of countless other life-saving drugs. The discovery of the electron in 1897 by J.J. Thomson paved the way for the development of electronics, which has transformed communication, transportation, and countless other aspects of modern life.

The process of scientific discovery is not a linear one. It is often a messy and unpredictable journey, with unexpected twists and turns along the way. Scientists may stumble upon new discoveries by accident, as was the case with penicillin, or they may spend years meticulously planning and executing experiments to test their hypotheses.

Sometimes, new discoveries come from unexpected sources. Citizen scientists, amateur astronomers, and even children have made significant contributions to scientific knowledge. For example, in 2019, a 17-year-old intern at NASA discovered a new planet orbiting a star 1,300 light-years away. This discovery demonstrates that anyone with curiosity and a passion for exploration can participate in the scientific enterprise.

Technology plays a crucial role in scientific discovery. New tools and techniques allow scientists to probe deeper into the mysteries of nature and to see things that were previously invisible. For example, the development of powerful telescopes has allowed us to see galaxies billions of light-years away, while the invention of microscopes has opened up a whole new world of microorganisms.

The advent of big data and artificial intelligence has also transformed scientific research. Scientists can now analyze vast amounts of data to identify patterns and trends that would be impossible to detect manually. This has led to breakthroughs in fields as diverse as genomics, astronomy, and climate science.

But technology is not a panacea. It is merely a tool, and its effectiveness depends on the skill and creativity of the scientists who use it. The most sophisticated instrument is useless without a curious mind to guide it and a thoughtful interpretation of the data it generates.

The scientific community plays a crucial role in the process of scientific change. Scientists are not lone wolves working in isolation; they are part of a global network of researchers who share their findings, challenge each other's ideas, and collaborate on new discoveries. This collaborative spirit is essential for the advancement of science, as it allows for the rigorous testing and validation of new ideas.

Peer review, the process by which scientific papers are evaluated by other scientists before publication, is a cornerstone of the scientific process. It ensures that scientific findings are robust and reliable, and it helps to prevent the spread of misinformation and pseudoscience.

Scientific change is not always smooth or without controversy. New discoveries can challenge deeply held beliefs and disrupt established paradigms. They can also raise ethical and social concerns, as we grapple with the implications of new technologies and their impact on our lives.

But it is precisely this ability to challenge and disrupt that makes science so powerful. By constantly questioning our assumptions and seeking new knowledge, we push the boundaries of human understanding and open up new possibilities for the future.

In the end, science is not about certainty; it is about embracing uncertainty and constantly striving to improve our understanding of the world. New discoveries are the fuel that drives this process, leading to new ideas, new technologies, and new ways of seeing ourselves and our place in the universe.

ppp

"Science is important because it helps us understand the world around us. It's like having a secret decoder ring that unlocks the mysteries of nature."

TEN

WHY IS SCIENCE IMPORTANT? IT HELPS US UNDERSTAND AND IMPROVE OUR WORLD.

In the vast tapestry of human knowledge, science stands as a shining beacon, illuminating the path towards understanding and improving our world. It is not merely a collection of facts or a set of equations; it is a way of thinking, a process of inquiry, and a powerful tool for solving problems and creating a better future. Science is essential for our survival, our progress, and our well-being. It is the engine that drives innovation, the foundation upon which we build our civilizations, and the key to unlocking the mysteries of the universe.

At its core, science is about understanding the world around us. It is the systematic study of the natural world through observation, experimentation, and analysis. It seeks to answer fundamental questions about how things work, why they happen, and what their consequences might be. This understanding is not merely an intellectual pursuit; it is essential for our survival and well-being.

Understanding the natural world allows us to predict and mitigate natural disasters. By studying earthquakes, volcanoes, hurricanes, and other phenomena, scientists can develop early warning systems, build stronger infrastructure, and implement evacuation plans that can save countless lives. Understanding the spread of diseases allows us to develop vaccines, treatments, and public health measures that protect us from pandemics and other health threats.

Science also helps us understand the complex systems that sustain life on Earth. By studying the interactions between the atmosphere, oceans, land, and living organisms, scientists can develop models to predict how these systems will respond to changes in the environment, such as climate change. This knowledge is essential for developing sustainable practices that protect our planet and ensure the well-being of future generations.

Beyond understanding the natural world, science is also about improving our world. Scientific discoveries and technological innovations have transformed our lives in countless ways, from the development of life-saving medicines and vaccines to the creation of new energy sources and communication technologies. Science has given us the tools to solve problems, to create new opportunities, and to build a better future.

The development of modern medicine is a testament to the power of science to improve human health. Vaccines have eradicated smallpox and polio, antibiotics have saved countless lives from bacterial infections, and medical imaging technologies have revolutionized diagnosis and treatment. Scientific research continues to push the boundaries of medical knowledge, offering hope for cures for cancer, Alzheimer's disease, and other debilitating conditions.

Science has also revolutionized agriculture, increasing food production and improving nutrition for millions of people worldwide. Through genetic engineering and crop breeding, scientists have developed crops that are more resistant to pests and diseases, require less water, and produce higher yields. This has helped to reduce hunger and malnutrition in many parts of the world.

In the field of energy, science has enabled us to harness new sources of power, such as solar, wind, and geothermal energy. These renewable energy sources offer a cleaner and more sustainable alternative to fossil fuels, which are major contributors to climate change. Scientific research is also exploring new ways to store and transmit energy, making it possible to power our homes, businesses, and transportation systems with clean energy.

Science is not just about practical applications; it is also about expanding our horizons and enriching our lives. Scientific discoveries have revealed the vastness and complexity of the universe, from the smallest subatomic particles to the largest structures in the cosmos. They have shown us the beauty and diversity of life on Earth, from the microscopic organisms that inhabit our bodies to the majestic whales that roam the oceans.

Science also inspires us to think critically, to question assumptions, and to embrace new ideas. It teaches us to value evidence, to be skeptical of claims that lack supporting data, and to be open to the possibility that our current understanding of the world may be incomplete or even incorrect. This critical thinking is essential for making informed decisions in our personal and professional lives, and for participating in the democratic process as informed citizens.

Science is not without its challenges. The pursuit of knowledge can be fraught with ethical dilemmas, as we grapple with the implications of new technologies and their potential impact on society. Scientific discoveries can also challenge deeply held beliefs and values, leading to controversy and debate.

However, these challenges are also opportunities for growth and reflection. By engaging in open and honest dialogue, by upholding ethical principles, and by prioritizing the well-being of humanity and the planet, we can ensure that science remains a force for good in the world.

In the end, science is not just a subject to be studied in school or a career path to be pursued. It is a way of life, a way of thinking, and a way of understanding the world around us. It is the key to unlocking our full potential as individuals and as a society. By embracing science, we embrace our curiosity, our creativity, and our capacity for innovation. We open ourselves up to a world of possibilities, and we empower ourselves to create a better future for all.

ᗁᗁᗁ

"You don't need a lab coat to be a scientist. Just by looking around, asking questions, and trying things out, you're already a part of the scientific adventure!"

ELEVEN

How can I be a scientist? By observing, questioning, and experimenting.

Have you ever looked up at the stars and wondered what they are made of? Or watched a bird soar through the sky and questioned how it stays aloft? Perhaps you've examined a flower and pondered its intricate design. If so, you've already begun your journey toward becoming a scientist. The path to scientific discovery is paved with curiosity, observation, questioning, and experimentation. These are the fundamental tools that empower us to explore the world around us, uncover its secrets, and contribute to our collective knowledge.

Observation: The Art of Seeing

Observation is the cornerstone of scientific inquiry. It is the act of paying close attention to the world around us, noticing details, patterns, and anomalies. Scientists are keen observers, constantly scanning their surroundings for clues that might lead to new discoveries. They use all their senses – sight, hearing, touch, smell, and even taste – to gather information about the natural world.

Observation is not just about passively looking at things; it is about actively engaging with the world. Scientists use a variety of tools to enhance their powers of observation, from microscopes and telescopes to sensors and cameras. They also develop their own observational skills through practice and training, learning to identify subtle cues and interpret complex patterns.

The art of observation is not just about seeing what is there; it is also about seeing what is not there. Scientists are trained to look for gaps in knowledge, to identify unanswered questions, and to challenge existing assumptions. They are not afraid to ask "why?" and "how?" and they are constantly seeking new ways to explore the world around them.

Questioning: The Fuel of Curiosity

Questioning is the fuel that drives scientific inquiry. It is the act of asking "why?" and "how?" about the things we observe. Scientists are not content with simply accepting things at face value; they want to understand the underlying mechanisms that drive the natural world.

Questions can arise from observations, from previous research, or from simple curiosity. They can be broad and open-ended, like "What is the origin of the universe?" or narrow and focused, like "How does this particular gene affect plant growth?" Regardless of their scope, questions are the starting point of scientific investigation.

Asking good questions is a skill that can be developed through practice and training. Scientists learn to frame their questions in a way that can be tested through experimentation or observation. They also learn to refine their questions as they gather more information and deepen their understanding of the topic.

Experimentation: The Test of Ideas

Experimentation is the process of testing hypotheses, which are educated guesses about how the world works. Scientists design experiments to isolate and manipulate variables in order to observe their effects. By systematically changing one variable at a time and observing the results, scientists can determine whether their hypotheses are supported or not.

Experiments can be simple or complex, depending on the nature of the question being asked. They can be conducted in a laboratory, in the field, or even in space. The key is to design experiments that are rigorous, repeatable, and controlled for potential sources of error.

The results of experiments are not always what scientists expect. Sometimes, experiments fail to support the initial hypothesis, leading to new questions and new avenues of research. Other times, experiments may produce unexpected results that challenge existing theories and lead to major breakthroughs.

Regardless of the outcome, experimentation is an essential part of the scientific process. It is the way we test our ideas against the real world and learn from our successes and failures.

The Cycle of Scientific Discovery

The process of observation, questioning, and experimentation is not a linear one. It is a continuous cycle, where new discoveries lead to new questions, which in turn lead to new experiments and new discoveries. This cycle of inquiry is what drives scientific progress and allows us to deepen our understanding of the world around us.

As scientists gather more information and refine their understanding of a particular phenomenon, they may revise their hypotheses or develop new ones. They may also discover new questions that were not previously apparent. This iterative process allows science to evolve and adapt as new evidence emerges.

The Importance of Collaboration and Communication

Science is not a solitary pursuit. It is a collaborative endeavor that relies on the sharing of ideas and the exchange of information. Scientists work together to design experiments, collect data, analyze results, and interpret findings. They also communicate their results to other scientists and to the public through publications, presentations, and outreach programs.

Collaboration and communication are essential for the advancement of science. They allow scientists to build upon each other's work, to challenge each other's ideas, and to collectively advance our understanding of the world. They also help to ensure the quality and rigor of scientific research, as findings are subject to peer review and scrutiny by other scientists.

How to Be a Scientist

Becoming a scientist is not about memorizing facts or mastering complex equations. It is about cultivating a curious mind, developing observational skills, asking good questions, and designing and conducting experiments. It is also about collaborating with others and communicating findings effectively.

Here are some tips for aspiring scientists:

Be curious. Ask questions about the world around you and seek

answers through observation and experimentation.

Be observant. Pay close attention to details, patterns, and anomalies.

Ask good questions. Frame your questions in a way that can be tested through experimentation or observation.

Design and conduct experiments. Learn to isolate and manipulate variables to observe their effects.

Analyze data. Look for patterns, trends, and relationships in your data.

Communicate your findings. Share your results with others through publications, presentations, or outreach programs.

Collaborate with others. Work with other scientists to design experiments, collect data, and interpret findings.

Remember, science is a journey, not a destination. There is always more to learn, more to discover, and more to understand. By embracing the power of observation, questioning, and experimentation, you can become a part of this exciting journey and contribute to our collective knowledge of the world.

ᐅᐅᐅ

"Nature is the most incredible playground you'll ever find. From tiny insects to giant planets, it's filled with amazing things to discover."

TWELVE
WHAT IS NATURE? THE INCREDIBLE WORLD AROUND US, FROM PLANTS TO PLANETS.

The word "nature" evokes a sense of wonder and awe. It encompasses the vast and intricate tapestry of life, the breathtaking landscapes, the awe-inspiring phenomena, and the intricate web of connections that bind all living things together. From the smallest microorganisms to the largest galaxies, nature is a symphony of diversity, complexity, and beauty.

In its simplest form, nature can be defined as the physical world and all its phenomena. It is the air we breathe, the water we drink, the soil that nourishes our crops, the sun that warms our planet, and the moon that illuminates our nights. It is the mountains that pierce the sky, the oceans that teem with life, the forests that provide shelter and sustenance, and the deserts that test the limits of survival.

But nature is much more than just the physical environment. It is also the living organisms that inhabit this world, from the tiniest bacteria to the largest whales. It is the intricate web of relationships between these organisms, the way they interact with each other and with their environment. It is the complex ecosystems that sustain life, from the coral reefs of the tropics to the tundra of the Arctic.

Nature is a source of endless fascination and inspiration. It has captivated the minds of poets, artists, philosophers, and scientists throughout history. Its beauty has been immortalized in paintings, poems, and songs. Its mysteries have been explored through scientific inquiry and philosophical reflection. And its power has been harnessed for human use, providing us with food, shelter, medicine, and countless other resources.

The diversity of nature is truly astonishing. There are millions of different species of plants and animals on Earth, each with its own unique adaptations and ecological role. From the vibrant colors of tropical birds to the intricate patterns of butterfly wings, nature's artistry is evident in every corner of the globe.

But nature is not just about beauty and diversity. It is also about power and resilience. The forces of nature can be both creative and destructive. Earthquakes, volcanoes, hurricanes, and floods can cause widespread devastation, but they also play a role in shaping the Earth's landscape and creating new habitats for life.

Nature is also a source of profound interconnectedness. Every living thing is part of a complex web of relationships, where the actions of one organism can have ripple effects on others. The food chain, the water cycle, and the carbon cycle are just a few examples of the intricate systems that sustain life on Earth.

Humans are an integral part of nature. We depend on nature for our survival, and our actions have a profound impact on the environment. We have the power to protect or destroy the natural world, and the choices we make today will determine the fate of future generations.

The importance of nature cannot be overstated. It provides us with the resources we need to survive, such as food, water, and clean air. It regulates the climate, protects us from natural disasters, and provides us with a sense of peace and well-being. It is the source of our inspiration, our creativity, and our spirituality.

Yet, despite its importance, nature is under threat. Human activities, such as deforestation, pollution, and climate change, are causing widespread damage to the environment and threatening the survival of many species. The loss of biodiversity, the depletion of natural resources, and the degradation of ecosystems are just a few of the consequences of our unsustainable practices.

Protecting nature is not just a matter of preserving its beauty or its diversity. It is about ensuring our own survival and well-being. By protecting nature, we are protecting ourselves, our children, and future generations. We are also preserving the natural heritage that has sustained life on Earth for billions of years.

There are many ways to protect nature. We can reduce our consumption of resources, recycle and reuse materials, support sustainable businesses, and advocate for policies that protect the environment. We can also get involved in conservation efforts, volunteer our time to clean up our communities, and educate others about the importance of nature.

Nature is a gift, a treasure trove of wonders that we are fortunate to inherit. It is our responsibility to protect and cherish this gift, to ensure that future generations can experience the same awe and inspiration that we feel when we witness the majesty of nature.

By recognizing our interconnectedness with nature, by valuing its diversity and resilience, and by taking action to protect it, we can create a more sustainable and harmonious relationship with the natural world. We can ensure that nature continues to provide us with the resources we need to thrive, to inspire us with its beauty, and to enrich our lives in countless ways.

ᐅᐅᐅ

"Everything you see and touch is made of tiny building blocks called atoms. They're so small you can't see them, but they make up everything in the universe!"

THIRTEEN

WHAT IS MATTER? THE STUFF EVERYTHING IS MADE OF.

Look around you. Everything you see, touch, and interact with is made of matter. The chair you're sitting on, the air you're breathing, the book you're holding, even your own body – it's all matter. But what exactly is this fundamental substance that makes up the world around us?

At its most basic level, matter is anything that has mass and takes up space. Mass refers to the amount of stuff in an object, while space refers to the volume it occupies. This simple definition encompasses a vast and diverse range of substances, from the tiniest subatomic particles to the largest structures in the universe.

To understand matter, we must first delve into its building blocks. All matter is composed of tiny particles called atoms. Atoms are so small that they are invisible to the naked eye, yet they are the fundamental units from which all matter is constructed. Each atom consists of a nucleus, which contains protons and neutrons, and a surrounding cloud of electrons.

Protons and neutrons are relatively heavy particles located in the nucleus of an atom. Protons carry a positive electrical charge, while neutrons have no charge. The number of protons in an atom's nucleus determines its atomic number and defines what element it is. For example, all atoms with one proton are hydrogen, all atoms with two protons are helium, and so on.

Electrons are much lighter particles that orbit the nucleus in a cloud-like region. They carry a negative electrical charge, and their arrangement around the nucleus determines the chemical properties of an atom. Atoms can gain or lose electrons to form ions, which are charged particles that play important roles in chemical reactions.

Atoms can combine with each other to form molecules, which are groups of two or more atoms held together by chemical bonds. Molecules can be simple, like a water molecule (H_2O), which consists of two hydrogen atoms and one oxygen atom, or they can be complex, like a DNA molecule, which contains millions of atoms arranged in a specific sequence.

The properties of matter depend on the types of atoms and molecules it is made of, as well as how these atoms and molecules are arranged. For example, water is a liquid at room temperature because its molecules are loosely bound together and can move around freely. Iron, on the other hand, is a solid at room temperature because its atoms are tightly packed together in a rigid structure.

Matter exists in different states, also known as phases. The three most familiar states of matter are solids, liquids, and gases. In a solid, the atoms or molecules are tightly packed together and have a fixed shape and volume. In a liquid, the atoms or molecules are still close together but can move around freely, giving the liquid a definite volume but no fixed shape. In a gas, the atoms or molecules are widely spaced and move around rapidly, giving the gas no definite shape or volume.

The state of matter can change depending on temperature and pressure. For example, water can exist as a solid (ice), a liquid (water), or a gas (steam) depending on the temperature. The transitions between these states are called phase changes.

Matter can also undergo chemical changes, in which the atoms or molecules rearrange themselves to form new substances with different properties. For example, when iron rusts, the iron atoms combine with oxygen atoms from the air to form iron oxide, a new substance with a reddish-brown color and different properties from the original iron.

The study of matter and its properties is a vast and fascinating field, encompassing disciplines such as chemistry, physics, and materials science. Scientists have discovered an incredible diversity of matter, from the exotic particles created in particle accelerators to the complex molecules that make up living organisms.

Matter is not only the stuff of stars and planets; it is also the stuff of life. The complex molecules that make up our bodies are constantly interacting and changing, enabling us to move, grow, and think. The food we eat, the air we breathe, and the water we drink are all essential sources of matter that our bodies need to function.

Understanding matter is crucial for addressing many of the challenges facing our world today. For example, the development of new materials with specific properties can lead to breakthroughs in energy storage, transportation, and medicine. The study of matter at the atomic and molecular level can also help us understand the causes of diseases and develop new treatments.

The quest to understand matter is a never-ending journey. As scientists continue to probe the depths of the atom and explore the vastness of the cosmos, they are constantly uncovering new mysteries and pushing the boundaries of human knowledge. The more we learn about matter, the more we realize how much there is still to discover.

᠗᠗᠗

"Energy is the power that makes things happen. It's like magic, but it's real, and it's everywhere – from the warmth of the sun to the energy in your food."

FOURTEEN

WHAT IS ENERGY? THE POWER THAT MAKES THINGS HAPPEN.

Energy: The Pulse of the Universe, The Spark of Transformation

Energy. It's a word we hear all the time, a concept that permeates every aspect of our existence. But what exactly is this elusive force that powers our world and makes things happen?

In its essence, energy is the capacity to do work or cause change. It's the invisible hand that sets the universe in motion, the driving force behind every action, every reaction, every transformation. From the smallest subatomic particles to the grandest cosmic events, energy is the pulse of the universe, the spark of creation.

Energy manifests itself in many forms, each with its own unique properties and characteristics. Kinetic energy is the energy of motion, the energy possessed by objects in motion. A speeding car, a soaring bird, a spinning top – they all possess kinetic energy. The faster an object moves and the more massive it is, the more kinetic energy it has.

Potential energy is the energy stored within an object due to its position or state. A rock perched on a cliff, a stretched rubber band, a battery – they all possess potential energy. This energy is not actively being used, but it has the potential to be converted into kinetic energy or other forms of energy.

Thermal energy, also known as heat, is the energy associated with the random motion of atoms and molecules. The hotter an object is, the faster its atoms and molecules move, and the more thermal energy it has. Thermal energy can be transferred from one object to another through conduction, convection, or radiation.

Chemical energy is the energy stored in the bonds between atoms and molecules. This energy is released or absorbed during chemical reactions, such as the burning of fuel or the digestion of food. Chemical energy is a crucial source of energy for living organisms, as it powers many of the processes that sustain life.

Electrical energy is the energy associated with the flow of electric charge. It is a versatile form of energy that can be easily converted into other forms, such as light, heat, or motion. Electrical energy powers our homes, our businesses, and our transportation systems.

Nuclear energy is the energy stored in the nucleus of an atom. This energy can be released through nuclear reactions, such as fission (the splitting of atomic nuclei) or fusion (the combining of atomic nuclei). Nuclear energy is a powerful but controversial source of energy, as it has the potential for both immense benefit and catastrophic harm.

The different forms of energy are not isolated; they can be transformed from one form to another. This principle, known as the conservation of energy, states that energy cannot be created or destroyed, only converted from one form to another. For example, when you turn on a light bulb, electrical energy is converted into light and heat. When you eat a piece of bread, the chemical energy stored in the bread is converted into kinetic energy that your body uses to move and function.

The concept of energy is central to our understanding of the universe. It underpins all physical and chemical processes, from the formation of stars and galaxies to the metabolism of a single cell. It is the driving force behind weather patterns, geological events, and the evolution of life.

Energy is also a fundamental concept in engineering and technology. Engineers use their knowledge of energy to design and build machines, power plants, and transportation systems. They also use energy to solve problems, such as finding new ways to generate electricity or developing more efficient ways to use energy.

Energy is a complex and multifaceted concept, but its importance is undeniable. It is the power that makes things happen, the force that drives the universe. By understanding the different forms of energy and how they interact, we can unlock the secrets of nature, harness its power for our benefit, and create a more sustainable and prosperous future for all.

ᐅᐅᐅ

"Matter can be a solid like ice, a liquid like water, or a gas like the air you breathe. It's like a shapeshifter, but it's all made of the same tiny building blocks."

FIFTEEN

WHAT ARE THE STATES OF MATTER? SOLID, LIQUID, AND GAS.

The world around us is a symphony of matter in motion, a dance of molecules that shapes the very fabric of our existence. But this dance is not a chaotic jumble; it follows a set of rules, a choreography that determines the states in which matter can exist. These states, known as solid, liquid, and gas, are the fundamental forms in which matter can manifest itself, each with its own distinct characteristics and properties.

At the heart of this dance lies the concept of molecular motion. The molecules that make up all matter are in constant motion, vibrating, rotating, and translating through space. The speed and freedom of this motion determine the state of matter.

In a solid, the molecules are tightly packed together, held in place by strong intermolecular forces. They can vibrate around fixed positions, but they cannot move past each other. This gives solids a definite shape and volume. Think of a brick: its shape and size remain constant, no matter how you turn it or where you place it.

Examples of solids are all around us: the chair you're sitting on, the book you're holding, the ice cubes in your drink. Solids are characterized by their rigidity, their resistance to deformation, and their ability to maintain their shape under pressure.

In a liquid, the molecules are still close together, but they have more freedom of movement than in a solid. They can slide past each other, allowing the liquid to flow and take the shape of its container. However, the intermolecular forces are still strong enough to hold the molecules together, giving the liquid a definite volume. Think of water in a glass: it takes the shape of the glass, but its volume remains constant.

Examples of liquids include water, oil, milk, and blood. Liquids are characterized by their fluidity, their ability to flow and take the shape of their container, and their relatively incompressibility. They can also exhibit surface tension, a phenomenon that allows insects to walk on water and water droplets to form on a leaf.

In a gas, the molecules are widely spaced and move around rapidly, colliding with each other and with the walls of their container. The intermolecular forces are weak, so the molecules have a high degree of freedom of movement. Gases have no definite shape or volume; they expand to fill the entire container they are in. Think of the air we breathe: it fills our lungs and expands to fill a room.

Examples of gases include air, oxygen, nitrogen, and carbon dioxide. Gases are characterized by their low density, their compressibility, and their ability to diffuse, or spread out, to fill any available space. They also exert pressure on the walls of their container, a phenomenon that we experience as atmospheric pressure.

The transitions between these states of matter are called phase changes. When a solid is heated, its molecules gain energy and start to vibrate faster. If enough heat is added, the intermolecular forces weaken, and the molecules can start to move past each other, turning the solid into a liquid. This process is called melting.

If a liquid is heated further, its molecules gain even more energy and move even faster. Eventually, the intermolecular forces become so weak that the molecules escape into the air, turning the liquid into a gas. This process is called evaporation or boiling, depending on the temperature at which it occurs.

Conversely, when a gas is cooled, its molecules lose energy and slow down. If enough heat is removed, the intermolecular forces strengthen, and the molecules start to clump together, turning the gas into a liquid. This process is called condensation.

If a liquid is cooled further, its molecules lose even more energy and move even slower. Eventually, the intermolecular forces become strong enough to lock the molecules into fixed positions, turning the liquid into a solid. This process is called freezing.

The states of matter are not limited to solids, liquids, and gases. There are also other states, such as plasma, which is a high-energy state of matter found in stars and lightning bolts. However, for most everyday purposes, the three states of matter we have discussed are the most relevant.

Understanding the states of matter is essential for many aspects of science and engineering. It helps us understand how materials behave under different conditions, how chemical reactions occur, and how energy is transferred. It is also essential for understanding the processes that shape our planet, from the movement of glaciers to the formation of clouds.

The states of matter are a reminder of the dynamic nature of the universe. The molecules that make up all matter are in constant motion, and their behavior determines the properties of the materials we interact with every day. By understanding the states of matter, we can gain a deeper appreciation for the complexity and beauty of the world around us.

ᕹᕹᕹ

"Energy comes in many different forms, like the light from a lamp, the heat from a fire, or the sound of your favorite song. It's all around us, making the world a vibrant and exciting place."

SIXTEEN

WHAT ARE THE DIFFERENT TYPES OF ENERGY? LIGHT, HEAT, SOUND, AND MORE!

Energy is the lifeblood of the universe, a force that manifests itself in countless ways, each with its own unique characteristics and effects. It's the warmth of the sun on our skin, the crackling of a fire, the rumble of thunder, the hum of a refrigerator, and the dazzling colors of a rainbow. Energy is everywhere, in everything, and it takes many different forms.

Light: The Illuminator

Light, or radiant energy, is the most familiar form of energy to us. It's the energy that allows us to see the world around us, from the vibrant colors of a sunset to the twinkling stars in the night sky. Light is a form of electromagnetic radiation, which is a type of energy that travels in waves.

These waves vary in wavelength and frequency, and different wavelengths correspond to different colors of light. Red light has the longest wavelength and lowest frequency, while violet light has the shortest wavelength and highest frequency. The entire range of wavelengths is known as the electromagnetic spectrum, which includes radio waves, microwaves, infrared radiation, visible light, ultraviolet radiation, X-rays, and gamma rays.

Light energy plays a crucial role in many natural processes. It is the energy source for photosynthesis, the process by which plants convert sunlight into chemical energy. It also drives the Earth's climate, as sunlight warms the planet's surface and drives atmospheric circulation.

Heat: The Energizer

Heat, or thermal energy, is the energy associated with the random motion of atoms and molecules. The hotter an object is, the faster its atoms and molecules move, and the more thermal energy it has. Heat can be transferred from one object to another through conduction, convection, or radiation.

Conduction is the transfer of heat through direct contact between objects. When you touch a hot stove, heat is transferred from the stove to your hand through conduction. Convection is the transfer of heat through the movement of fluids, such as air or water. When you turn on a heater, the warm air rises and circulates throughout the room, transferring heat through convection. Radiation is the transfer of heat through electromagnetic waves. The sun's heat reaches Earth through radiation.

Heat energy is essential for life. It keeps our bodies warm, cooks our food, and powers our industries. It is also a major factor in weather patterns and climate change.

Sound: The Vibrator

Sound is a form of mechanical energy that travels in waves through a medium, such as air or water. When an object vibrates, it creates sound waves that travel outward from the source. The pitch of a sound is determined by the frequency of the waves, while the loudness is determined by their amplitude.

Sound energy is used for communication, navigation, and entertainment. Humans use sound to speak and listen, animals use it to attract mates and warn of danger, and bats use it to echolocate their prey. Sound is also used in music, movies, and other forms of entertainment.

Other Forms of Energy

In addition to light, heat, and sound, there are many other forms of energy. Mechanical energy is the energy of motion and position. It includes both kinetic energy (the energy of motion) and potentialenergy (the energy of position).

Electrical energy is the energy associated with the flow of electric charge. It is a versatile form of energy that can be easily converted into other forms, such as light, heat, or motion.

Chemical energy is the energy stored in the bonds between atoms and molecules. This energy is released or absorbed during chemical reactions, such as the burning of fuel or the digestion of food.

Nuclear energy is the energy stored in the nucleus of an atom. This energy can be released through nuclear reactions, such as fission (the splitting of atomic nuclei) or fusion (the combining of atomic nuclei).

Gravitational energy is the energy associated with the force of gravity. It is the energy that holds planets in orbit around stars and galaxies together.

Renewable and Non-Renewable Energy

Energy sources can be classified as either renewable or non-renewable. Renewable energy sources are those that can be replenished naturally over time, such as solar, wind, hydro, geothermal, and biomass energy. Non-renewable energy sources are those that are finite and will eventually run out, such as coal, oil, and natural gas.

The use of non-renewable energy sources has led to a number of environmental problems, including climate change, air pollution, and water pollution. As a result, there is a growing interest in developing and using renewable energy sources.

The Future of Energy

Energy is essential for modern life, but our current reliance on non-renewable energy sources is unsustainable. The transition to a more sustainable energy future will require a combination of technological innovation, policy changes, and individual action.

Scientists and engineers are working to develop new technologies that can harness renewable energy sources more efficiently and affordably. Policymakers are enacting policies to encourage the development and use of renewable energy. And individuals can make a difference by reducing their energy consumption, supporting renewable energy initiatives, and educating others about the importance of a sustainable energy future.

ppp

"Scientific theories are like giant puzzle pieces. They help us understand how the big picture of the universe fits together."

SEVENTEEN

WHAT ARE ATOMS? THE TINY BUILDING BLOCKS OF EVERYTHING.

Atoms: The Fundamental Building Blocks of the Universe

Gazing at the vast expanse of the night sky, it's easy to feel overwhelmed by the sheer scale and complexity of the universe. Yet, beneath this cosmic grandeur lies a fundamental truth: everything we see, touch, and interact with is built from tiny, indivisible particles called atoms. These microscopic entities are the fundamental building blocks of matter, the basic units from which all substances are constructed.

To truly grasp the significance of atoms, imagine a Lego set with an endless supply of bricks. These bricks are the atoms, and the structures you build with them represent the diverse array of matter that exists in the universe. Just as you can create an infinite variety of structures with Lego bricks, so too can atoms combine in countless ways to form the matter that makes up stars, planets, oceans, mountains, trees, animals, and even ourselves.

Atoms are incredibly small, typically measuring less than one ten-billionth of a meter across. To put this in perspective, a single human hair is about a million carbon atoms wide. Yet, despite their minuscule size, atoms are incredibly complex, composed of even smaller subatomic particles: protons, neutrons, and electrons.

At the center of every atom lies the nucleus, a dense core that contains protons and neutrons. Protons carry a positive electrical charge, while neutrons have no charge. The number of protons in an atom's nucleus determines its atomic number and defines what element it is. For example, all atoms with one proton are hydrogen, all atoms with two protons are helium, and so on.

Surrounding the nucleus is a cloud of electrons, which are negatively charged particles that orbit the nucleus at high speeds. The number of electrons in an atom is usually equal to the number of protons, ensuring that the atom is electrically neutral. The arrangement of electrons in an atom's electron cloud determines its chemical properties and how it interacts with other atoms.

The behavior of atoms is governed by the laws of quantum mechanics, a branch of physics that describes the behavior of matter and energy at the atomic and subatomic level. Quantum mechanics reveals that the world of atoms is a strange and counterintuitive place, where particles can exist in multiple states simultaneously and where the act of observation can alter the outcome of an experiment.

Despite their complexity, atoms are remarkably stable. The strong force that binds protons and neutrons together in the nucleus is one of the most powerful forces in nature, ensuring that atoms remain intact even under extreme conditions. However, atoms can also undergo changes, such as radioactive decay, in which an unstable nucleus emits particles or radiation.

Atoms can also combine with each other to form molecules, which are groups of two or more atoms held together by chemical bonds. These bonds are formed by the sharing or transfer of electrons between atoms. Molecules can be simple, like a water molecule (H_2O), which consists of two hydrogen atoms and one oxygen atom, or they can be complex, like a DNA molecule, which contains millions of atoms arranged in a specific sequence.

The diversity of matter that exists in the universe is a testament to the versatility of atoms. By combining in different ways and in different proportions, atoms can form an infinite variety of substances with unique properties. For example, the simple combination of carbon, hydrogen, and oxygen can form a wide range of molecules, from sugars and starches to fats and proteins.

The study of atoms has revolutionized our understanding of the world. It has led to the development of new materials, new technologies, and new medicines. By understanding the structure and behavior of atoms, scientists have been able to manipulate matter at the atomic level, creating new substances with properties that were previously unimaginable.

The quest to understand atoms is far from over. Scientists are still exploring the mysteries of the atomic world, searching for new particles, new forces, and new ways to harness the power of atoms. The future of science and technology is inextricably linked to our understanding of atoms, as we continue to explore the fundamental building blocks of the universe.

ppp

"Science is a gift that keeps on giving. It helps us understand the world, invent new things, and make life better for everyone."

EIGHTEEN

HOW DO WE MEASURE THINGS? SCIENTISTS USE TOOLS LIKE RULERS AND SCALES.

From the earliest days of human civilization, we have sought to understand and quantify the world around us. We have measured the length of a day, the distance to the moon, the weight of a grain of sand, and the temperature of a star. Measurement is a fundamental human activity, a way of making sense of the world and communicating our observations to others.

At its core, measurement is the process of assigning numbers to physical quantities. We measure length, mass, time, temperature, electric current, and many other quantities. These measurements allow us to compare different objects, to quantify changes over time, and to make predictions about the future.

The tools of measurement are as diverse as the quantities they measure. Rulers and tape measures are used to measure length, scales and balances are used to measure mass, clocks and stopwatches are used to measure time, thermometers are used to measure temperature, and ammeters and voltmeters are used to measure electric current.

But measurement is more than just using tools; it is also about understanding the principles that underpin the act of measurement. These principles include the concept of units, the importance of accuracy and precision, and the role of uncertainty in measurement.

Units: The Language of Measurement

Units are the standard quantities against which we compare other quantities. For example, the meter is the standard unit of length, the kilogram is the standard unit of mass, and the second is the standard unit of time. By using standard units, we can ensure that our measurements are consistent and comparable, regardless of who makes them or where they are made.

The International System of Units (SI), also known as the metric system, is the most widely used system of measurement in the world. It is a decimal system, meaning that units are related to each other by powers of ten. For example, one kilometer is equal to 1,000 meters, and one milligram is equal to one-thousandth of a gram. This makes it easy to convert between different units and to perform calculations with measurements.

Accuracy and Precision: The Goals of Measurement

Accuracy and precision are two important concepts in measurement. Accuracy refers to how close a measurement is to the true value of the quantity being measured. Precision refers to how close repeated measurements of the same quantity are to each other.

For example, if you measure the length of a table multiple times and get slightly different results each time, your measurements are not very precise. However, if the average of your measurements is close to the true length of the table, your measurements are accurate.

The accuracy and precision of a measurement depend on several factors, including the quality of the measuring instrument, the skill of the person making the measurement, and the environmental conditions under which the measurement is made.

Uncertainty in Measurement: The Limits of Knowledge

No measurement is perfectly accurate or precise. There is always some degree of uncertainty associated with every measurement. This uncertainty can arise from limitations in the measuring instrument, variations in the quantity being measured, or human error.

Scientists and engineers are well aware of the limitations of measurement and take steps to minimize uncertainty. They use calibrated instruments, carefully control experimental conditions, and repeat measurements multiple times to ensure their results are reliable. They also report their measurements with an estimate of the uncertainty, such as a plus or minus range or a confidence interval.

The Role of Measurement in Science

Measurement is essential for scientific inquiry. It allows scientists to quantify natural phenomena, to test hypotheses, and to develop theories. Without measurement, science would be reduced to mere speculation and conjecture.

In physics, measurement is used to determine the fundamental constants of nature, such as the speed of light, the gravitational constant, and the Planck constant. These constants are the building blocks of physical theories, and their precise measurement is essential for understanding the universe.

In chemistry, measurement is used to determine the composition and properties of matter. Chemists use a variety of instruments to measure the mass, volume, temperature, and other properties of substances. This information is used to identify and classify substances, to study chemical reactions, and to develop new materials.

In biology, measurement is used to study living organisms and their interactions with the environment. Biologists use a variety of tools to measure the size, shape, growth, and behavior of organisms. This information is used to understand the diversity of life, to study the evolution of species, and to develop new medicines and treatments.

The Future of Measurement

The science of measurement is constantly evolving. New technologies are being developed that allow us to measure things with greater accuracy and precision than ever before. For example, atomic clocks are so precise that they lose less than one second every hundred million years.

ppp

"Every little thing you do can make a difference. By learning about science, you can be a hero for our planet and help create a brighter future for everyone."

NINETEEN

WHAT ARE SCIENTIFIC THEORIES? BIG IDEAS THAT EXPLAIN HOW THINGS WORK.

Scientific Theories: The Grand Frameworks That Illuminate Our Understanding of the Universe

In the realm of science, theories are not mere guesses or hunches. They are not fleeting notions that come and go with the wind. Instead, scientific theories are grand, overarching frameworks that weave together a tapestry of observations, experiments, and evidence to explain the fundamental workings of the natural world. They are the culmination of years, often decades or even centuries, of meticulous research and rigorous testing.

A scientific theory is not simply a hypothesis, which is an educated guess that can be tested through experimentation. Rather, a theory is a well-substantiated explanation that has been repeatedly confirmed through empirical evidence. It is a comprehensive and coherent framework that can explain a wide range of phenomena and predict new ones.

Consider the theory of gravity, one of the most well-established theories in science. It explains why objects fall to the ground, why planets orbit the sun, and why galaxies cluster together. It is not just a guess; it is a powerful explanation that has been tested and confirmed through countless experiments and observations.

The theory of evolution is another example of a scientific theory that has revolutionized our understanding of the world. It explains how life on Earth has changed over time, through the process of natural selection. It is supported by a vast body of evidence from fossils, genetics, and comparative anatomy.

Scientific theories are not static; they evolve and adapt as new evidence emerges. They are constantly being tested and refined, and sometimes they are even overturned if new evidence contradicts them. However, the most well-established theories, such as the theory of gravity and the theory of evolution, have withstood the test of time and continue to provide a solid foundation for our understanding of the natural world.

Theories are not just about explaining what we already know; they are also about predicting new phenomena. For example, Einstein's theory of general relativity predicted the existence of gravitational waves, ripples in spacetime caused by the movement of massive objects. These waves were finally detected in 2015, a century after Einstein first predicted their existence.

Theories also play a crucial role in guiding scientific research. They provide a framework for asking new questions and designing experiments to test those questions. For example, the theory of plate tectonics, which explains how the Earth's crust is divided into plates that move and interact with each other, has guided geologists in their search for new mineral deposits and their understanding of earthquakes and volcanoes.

Theories also have practical applications. The theory of electromagnetism, for example, has led to the development of countless technologies, from electric motors and generators to radios and televisions. The theory of quantum mechanics has led to the development of lasers, transistors, and other electronic devices that are essential to modern life.

The development of a scientific theory is a long and arduous process. It often begins with a single observation or a curious question. Scientists then conduct experiments, collect data, and analyze their findings. If the evidence supports their hypothesis, they may develop a theory to explain the phenomenon.

But a theory is not accepted by the scientific community until it has been rigorously tested and confirmed by multiple independent researchers. This process of peer review ensures that scientific theories are based on solid evidence and are not simply the product of wishful thinking or personal bias.

Once a theory is accepted, it becomes part of the scientific canon, a body of knowledge that is constantly being tested and refined. But even the most well-established theories are not immune to challenge. New discoveries can always lead to revisions or even the overthrow of existing theories.

This is the beauty of science: it is a self-correcting process that is always open to new ideas and new evidence. The scientific method ensures that our understanding of the world is constantly evolving, as we strive to unravel the mysteries of the universe.

The development and testing of scientific theories is a collaborative effort. Scientists from all over the world work together to share their findings, challenge each other's ideas, and build upon each other's work. This collaborative spirit is essential for the advancement of science, as it allows for the rigorous testing and validation of new ideas.

Scientific theories are not just for scientists; they are for everyone. They are a powerful tool for understanding the world around us and making informed decisions about our lives and our future. By learning about scientific theories, we can better appreciate the complexity and beauty of the universe, and we can become more engaged and informed citizens.

The next time you hear someone dismiss a scientific idea as "just a theory," remember that scientific theories are not mere guesses or hunches. They are the grand frameworks that illuminate our understanding of the universe, the culmination of years of research and rigorous testing. They are the most powerful explanations we have for how the world works.

ﭖﭖﭖ

"The world is a living laboratory, filled with experiments waiting to be conducted. Grab your magnifying glass, put on your thinking cap, and let the adventure begin!"

TWENTY
WHAT ARE SCIENTIFIC LAWS? RULES THAT DESCRIBE HOW NATURE BEHAVES.

Scientific Laws: Unveiling the Timeless Patterns of Nature

In the grand tapestry of the universe, there exist certain fundamental principles that govern the behavior of matter, energy, and the interactions between them. These principles, often expressed in the form of concise statements or mathematical equations, are known as scientific laws. They are not mere human constructs or arbitrary rules; they are the immutable truths that underpin the workings of nature, the timeless patterns that have shaped the cosmos since its inception.

Scientific laws are not to be confused with scientific theories, which are broader explanations of how and why things happen. While theories can evolve and change as new evidence emerges, laws are considered to be more fundamental and enduring. They describe the relationships between observable phenomena with remarkable precision and consistency.

The laws of motion, formulated by Isaac Newton in the 17th century, are perhaps the most famous examples of scientific laws. These laws describe how objects move in response to forces, and they have been instrumental in our understanding of everything from the motion of planets to the flight of airplanes. Newton's laws are so fundamental that they are still taught in schools today and form the basis of much of classical mechanics.

Another iconic scientific law is the law of conservation of energy, which states that energy cannot be created or destroyed, only transformed from one form to another. This law is a cornerstone of physics and has far-reaching implications for our understanding of the universe. It explains why a ball rolling down a hill eventually comes to a stop, why a light bulb glows when electricity flows through it, and why the sun shines.

The laws of thermodynamics are another set of fundamental laws that describe the relationship between heat, work, and energy. These laws have profound implications for our understanding of energy conversion and efficiency, and they play a crucial role in the design of engines, power plants, and other technological systems.

Scientific laws are not limited to physics. In chemistry, the law of definite proportions states that a given chemical compound always contains the same elements in the same proportion by mass. This law was instrumental in the development of the atomic theory, which revolutionized our understanding of matter.

In biology, the laws of genetics describe how traits are passed down from parents to offspring. These laws have been essential for our understanding of heredity, evolution, and the genetic basis of diseases.

The discovery of scientific laws is a testament to the power of human observation and reasoning. By carefully observing the natural world, scientists have been able to identify patterns and regularities that hold true across a wide range of phenomena. They have then used mathematics and logic to formulate these patterns into concise and precise statements or equations.

The discovery of scientific laws is not always a straightforward process. It often requires years of painstaking research, careful experimentation, and rigorous analysis of data. But the rewards are immense. Scientific laws provide us with a deep and profound understanding of the universe, allowing us to predict the behavior of natural systems and to harness the power of nature for our benefit.

Scientific laws are not just for scientists; they are for everyone. They are a powerful tool for understanding the world around us and making informed decisions about our lives and our future. By learning about scientific laws, we can better appreciate the complexity and beauty of the universe, and we can become more engaged and informed citizens.

The laws of nature are not subject to human whims or political ideologies. They are universal truths that transcend cultural and geographical boundaries. They remind us that we are part of a larger cosmic order, governed by principles that are far more powerful than any human invention.

In a world that is often chaotic and unpredictable, scientific laws offer a sense of order and stability. They remind us that there are underlying patterns and regularities that govern the universe, even if we do not always fully understand them. They offer a sense of hope and optimism, as they demonstrate that the universe is not random or chaotic, but rather follows a set of predictable and understandable rules.

Scientific laws are a testament to the power of human ingenuity and our insatiable thirst for knowledge. They are the culmination of centuries of inquiry, the fruit of countless experiments and observations. They are the keys that unlock the secrets of nature, the tools that allow us to understand and shape our world.

ppp

"Science is not about memorizing facts, but about understanding the connections between them. It's like weaving a tapestry, where each thread of knowledge contributes to the overall beauty and complexity of the picture."

TWENTY-ONE

HOW DOES SCIENCE HELP US? IT LEADS TO INVENTIONS THAT IMPROVE OUR LIVES.

From the flickering light of the first controlled fire to the dazzling displays of modern technology, the journey of human civilization has been inextricably intertwined with science. Science is not merely a theoretical pursuit; it is a dynamic force that shapes our world, fueling innovation and propelling us towards a future filled with possibilities. Through its relentless pursuit of knowledge and understanding, science has led to countless inventions that have profoundly improved our lives, transforming the way we live, work, communicate, and interact with the world around us.

At its core, science is about solving problems. It is the systematic study of the natural world, driven by a desire to understand how things work and why they happen. This understanding, in turn, allows us to develop new technologies and innovations that address the challenges we face.

Consider the field of medicine, where science has played a pivotal role in improving human health and longevity. Vaccines, antibiotics, and other life-saving drugs have been developed through scientific research, eradicating deadly diseases and extending lifespans. Medical imaging technologies, such as X-rays, MRI scans, and CT scans, have revolutionized diagnosis and treatment, allowing doctors to peer inside the human body and identify diseases at their earliest stages.

The development of these life-saving inventions was not a matter of chance; it was the result of years of painstaking research, experimentation, and collaboration. Scientists studied the human body, identified the causes of diseases, and developed treatments based on their understanding of biological processes. This knowledge, in turn, was translated into practical applications that have saved countless lives and improved the quality of life for millions.

In the realm of communication, science has brought about a revolution. The invention of the telephone, radio, television, and the internet has connected people across vast distances, enabling instant communication and the exchange of information on a global scale. These technologies have transformed the way we work, learn, and interact with each other, creating a more interconnected and globalized world.

The development of these communication technologies was not a linear process; it was a series of breakthroughs and innovations, each building upon the previous one. Scientists and engineers worked tirelessly to overcome technical challenges, develop new materials, and design more efficient systems. This relentless pursuit of innovation has led to the creation of tools that have become indispensable to modern life.

Transportation is another area where science has had a profound impact. The invention of the steam engine, the internal combustion engine, and the jet engine revolutionized travel, making it possible to transport people and goods over long distances quickly and efficiently. This has facilitated trade, tourism, and cultural exchange, bringing people from different parts of the world closer together.

The development of these transportation technologies was not without its challenges. It required the development of new materials, new fuels, and new engineering techniques. But through perseverance and ingenuity, scientists and engineers were able to overcome these challenges and create inventions that have transformed the way we travel and experience the world.

In the realm of energy, science has played a crucial role in developing new sources of power and improving energy efficiency. The harnessing of solar, wind, and geothermal energy has provided us with cleaner and more sustainable alternatives to fossil fuels, which are major contributors to climate change. The development of energy-efficient appliances, buildings, and transportation systems has also helped to reduce our reliance on fossil fuels and decrease our carbon footprint.

The quest for sustainable energy solutions is an ongoing challenge, but science is at the forefront of this effort. Researchers are developing new technologies to capture and store solar energy, to generate electricity from wind and waves, and to extract geothermal energy from the Earth's interior. These innovations hold the promise of a cleaner, greener, and more sustainable energy future.

Science has also had a profound impact on our understanding of the universe and our place within it. Through the use of telescopes, satellites, and other instruments, scientists have explored the vast expanse of space, discovering new planets, galaxies, and phenomena. They have also delved into the microscopic world, revealing the intricate structures and processes that govern life at the cellular and molecular level.

These discoveries have not only expanded our knowledge but have also inspired us to think differently about ourselves and our place in the cosmos. They have shown us that we are part of a vast and interconnected universe, a universe that is still full of mysteries waiting to be solved.

In conclusion, science is a powerful force that has transformed our world in countless ways. It has led to inventions that have improved our health, enriched our lives, and expanded our horizons. It has given us the tools to solve problems, to create new opportunities, and to build a better future.

The journey of scientific discovery is an ongoing one, with new breakthroughs and innovations emerging all the time. As we continue to explore the frontiers of knowledge, we can look forward to a future filled with even greater possibilities. Through science, we can unlock the secrets of nature, harness its power for our benefit, and create a world that is healthier, more sustainable, and more equitable for all.

ppp

"The scientific method is not a rigid set of rules, but a flexible framework for exploration. It's like a compass that can guide you through the uncharted territory of knowledge, leading you to unexpected discoveries."

TWENTY-TWO

WHY SHOULD WE PROTECT OUR PLANET? TO KEEP IT HEALTHY FOR US AND ALL LIVING THINGS.

Picture a vibrant tapestry teeming with life, a delicate balance of ecosystems where every living being plays a crucial role. This is our planet Earth, a unique and precious jewel in the vast cosmos. It is our home, the cradle of our civilization, and the source of all that sustains us. Protecting our planet is not merely an act of environmentalism; it is an act of self-preservation, a responsibility we owe to ourselves, to future generations, and to all living things that share this planet with us.

The Earth is a complex and interconnected system, where every element, from the smallest microorganism to the vast oceans, plays a vital role in maintaining the delicate balance of life. This balance is essential for our survival and well-being. It provides us with clean air to breathe, clean water to drink, fertile soil to grow our food, and a stable climate to support our communities.

The consequences of neglecting our planet's health are dire. Climate change, caused by the excessive accumulation of greenhouse gases in the atmosphere, is already wreaking havoc on our planet. Rising temperatures are leading to more frequent and intense heatwaves, droughts, floods, and wildfires, disrupting ecosystems, displacing communities, and threatening food security.

The loss of biodiversity, driven by habitat destruction, pollution, and overexploitation of resources, is another major threat to our planet's health. As species disappear, ecosystems become less resilient and more vulnerable to collapse. This loss of biodiversity not only impoverishes our planet, but it also threatens our own survival, as we depend on diverse ecosystems for food, medicine, and other essential resources.

Pollution, another consequence of human activity, is poisoning our air, water, and soil, harming wildlife, and threatening human health. Toxic chemicals, plastic waste, and other pollutants are accumulating in our environment, causing cancer, birth defects, and other serious health problems.

The unsustainable use of resources is also putting a strain on our planet's ability to support life. We are consuming resources at a rate that far exceeds the Earth's capacity to regenerate them, leading to deforestation, soil erosion, water scarcity, and other environmental problems.

Protecting our planet is not just an environmental issue; it is also a social justice issue. The impacts of environmental degradation are not evenly distributed. The poorest and most vulnerable communities are often the hardest hit by climate change, pollution, and resource depletion. They are the ones who lack the resources to adapt to a changing climate, to access clean water and sanitation, and to protect themselves from environmental hazards.

Protecting our planet is also an economic issue. A healthy planet is essential for a healthy economy. Environmental degradation can lead to economic losses through reduced agricultural productivity, increased healthcare costs, and damage to infrastructure. Investing in environmental protection is not only the right thing to do, it is also the smart thing to do.

The good news is that we have the power to protect our planet. By making conscious choices in our daily lives, we can reduce our environmental impact and contribute to a more sustainable future. We can reduce our consumption of resources, recycle and reuse materials, support renewable energy sources, and advocate for policies that protect the environment.

We can also get involved in community efforts to clean up our neighborhoods, plant trees, and create green spaces. We can educate others about the importance of environmental protection and inspire them to take action.

Protecting our planet is not just a matter of individual action; it also requires collective action. We need governments, businesses, and civil society to work together to address the complex challenges facing our planet. We need to develop and implement policies that promote sustainability, reduce emissions, and protect biodiversity.

We also need to invest in research and development to find new solutions to environmental problems. Scientists and engineers are working on innovative technologies that can help us reduce our reliance on fossil fuels, clean up pollution, and restore damaged ecosystems.

Protecting our planet is a monumental challenge, but it is one that we must rise to meet. The fate of our planet, and the future of all living things, depends on it. By working together, we can create a world where people and nature thrive, a world where future generations can enjoy the same clean air, clean water, and healthy ecosystems that we have been fortunate enough to inherit.

Protecting our planet is not just a duty; it is an opportunity. It is an opportunity to create a more just, equitable, and sustainable world. It is an opportunity to reconnect with nature and to rediscover our place in the web of life. It is an opportunity to build a legacy of hope and prosperity for generations to come.

"The greatest scientists are not always the ones with the most advanced degrees or the most sophisticated equipment. They are the ones with the most insatiable curiosity, the most relentless pursuit of truth, and the most unwavering belief in the power of human ingenuity."

TWENTY-THREE

HOW CAN I MAKE A DIFFERENCE? BY LEARNING ABOUT SCIENCE AND CARING FOR OUR WORLD.

The world we inhabit is a complex and interconnected system, where every action we take, no matter how small, can have far-reaching consequences. As inhabitants of this planet, we have a responsibility to care for it, to protect its resources, and to ensure its well-being for future generations. But how can we, as individuals, make a meaningful difference in the face of global challenges like climate change, pollution, and resource depletion? The answer lies in the power of knowledge, specifically scientific knowledge, and the empathy that fuels our desire to care for our world.

Science is not just a collection of facts and figures; it is a way of understanding the world, a framework for asking questions and seeking answers. By learning about science, we gain insights into the natural world and the complex systems that sustain life on Earth. We learn about the delicate balance of ecosystems, the impacts of human activities on the environment, and the potential consequences of our choices.

This knowledge is not just theoretical; it is empowering. It equips us with the tools we need to make informed decisions, to advocate for change, and to take action to protect our planet. Armed with scientific knowledge, we can understand the science behind climate change, the causes and consequences of pollution, and the importance of biodiversity. We can make informed choices about our consumption habits, our energy use, and our transportation choices. We can support policies that promote sustainability and advocate for solutions that address the root causes of environmental problems.

But knowledge alone is not enough. To truly make a difference, we must also cultivate a sense of care and responsibility for our world. This means recognizing that we are part of a larger ecosystem, interconnected with all living things. It means understanding that our actions have consequences, not just for ourselves, but for all life on Earth.

Caring for our world can take many forms. It can mean reducing our environmental footprint by conserving water, recycling, and using energy-efficient appliances. It can mean supporting organizations that are working to protect the environment and promote sustainability. It can mean educating others about the importance of environmental protection and inspiring them to take action.

It can also mean advocating for change at the local, national, and international levels. By speaking out against environmentally harmful practices, supporting policies that promote sustainability, and voting for leaders who prioritize environmental protection, we can help to create a more just and equitable world for all.

The power of individual action should not be underestimated. Every time we choose to walk or bike instead of drive, to buy locally sourced food, or to conserve water, we are making a difference. These small actions, multiplied by millions of people, can have a significant impact on the environment.

But individual action alone is not enough. We need systemic change to address the root causes of environmental problems. This means transforming our energy systems, our agricultural practices, and our consumption habits. It means creating a circular economy where resources are used efficiently and waste is minimized.

The role of science in achieving systemic change is crucial. Scientists are working tirelessly to develop new technologies that can help us reduce our environmental impact and create a more sustainable future. They are developing renewable energy sources, finding new ways to clean up pollution, and engineering materials that are less harmful to the environment.

But scientists cannot do it alone. They need the support of policymakers, businesses, and civil society to implement these solutions and to create the political will for change. This is where the power of a caring heart comes in. By raising our voices, by demanding action from our leaders, and by supporting organizations that are working to protect the environment, we can create the momentum needed for systemic change.

Making a difference is not just about doing big things; it is also about doing small things consistently. It is about making conscious choices in our daily lives, about being mindful of our impact on the environment, and about taking action to protect the planet we call home.

By learning about science and caring for our world, we can create a ripple of change that will extend far beyond our individual lives. We can inspire others to take action, we can influence policy, and we can contribute to a more sustainable and equitable future for all. The power to make a difference is in our hands; let us use it wisely.

ppp

"Science is not just a subject to be studied; it is a way of life. It is a way of looking at the world with wonder and curiosity, a way of questioning assumptions and seeking evidence, a way of embracing the unknown and challenging the limits of our understanding."

TWENTY-FOUR
SUMMARY

Science is a thrilling journey of exploration and discovery, driven by our insatiable curiosity about the world around us. It is not merely a collection of facts and figures, but a dynamic process of asking questions, seeking answers, and continuously refining our understanding of the universe.

At its core, science is about asking "why?" and "how?" Why does the sky change color at sunset? How do birds know where to migrate? What causes earthquakes and volcanoes? These questions and countless others have fueled our quest for knowledge and led to countless discoveries that have transformed our lives.

To answer these questions, scientists use a variety of tools and techniques, from simple observations and experiments to complex computer simulations and mathematical models. They employ the scientific method, a systematic approach that involves asking questions, formulating hypotheses, designing experiments, collecting data, analyzing results, and drawing conclusions. This rigorous process ensures that scientific findings are based on solid evidence and are not simply the product of speculation or bias.

One of the most fundamental concepts in science is matter, the stuff that everything is made of. Matter exists in different states – solid, liquid, and gas – depending on the arrangement and movement of its constituent particles, called atoms. Atoms are the tiny building blocks of matter, and they can combine in countless ways to form the diverse array of substances that we see around us.

Energy is another fundamental concept in science. It is the capacity to do work or cause change, and it comes in many forms, including light, heat, sound, and electricity. Energy is essential for life and for all the processes that occur in the universe.

The study of science has led to countless inventions that have improved our lives in innumerable ways. From life-saving medicines and vaccines to innovative technologies that connect us across the globe, science has transformed the way we live, work, and interact with the world. It has also helped us to understand the complex systems that sustain life on Earth and to develop solutions to environmental problems such as climate change and pollution.

Science is not just for scientists; it is for everyone. By learning about science, we can become more informed citizens, capable of making sound decisions about our health, our environment, and our future. We can also participate in the scientific enterprise by asking questions, conducting experiments, and sharing our findings with others.

But science is not just about knowledge; it is also about responsibility. As we learn more about the world, we must also consider the ethical implications of our discoveries and use our knowledge for the betterment of humanity and the planet. We must recognize that we are part of a larger ecosystem and that our actions have consequences for all living things.

Protecting our planet is not just an environmental issue; it is a moral imperative. The Earth is our only home, and we have a responsibility to care for it. By reducing our environmental footprint, supporting sustainable practices, and advocating for policies that protect the environment, we can ensure that future generations inherit a healthy and habitable planet.

Science is a journey of discovery, a quest for knowledge that has the power to transform our world. By embracing the spirit of inquiry, by asking questions, seeking answers, and taking action to protect our planet, we can all make a difference. The future of our world depends on it.

ᎦᎦᎦ

"The Earth is our home, and it's up to us to protect it. By learning about science and caring for our planet, we can make sure it's healthy for us and for all living things."

Citation And References

This book represents the culmination of extensive research and meticulous analysis, incorporating a diverse range of sources, including numerous books, scholarly studies, and personal experiences. Additionally, I have scoured various websites to gather relevant information and data essential for the compilation of this work. I have taken every precaution to ensure the accuracy of the information presented and have diligently cited all sources to acknowledge their contributions.

Despite these efforts, the possibility of inadvertent errors remains. I deeply value the insights of my readers and appreciate any feedback that can help identify and rectify such inaccuracies. I encourage you to bring any discrepancies to my attention.

Your feedback is not only welcome but crucial, as it will aid in correcting current editions and enhancing the content of future ones. I am committed to maintaining the highest standards of accuracy and reliability in my work and thank you for your support and understanding.

Additionally, I firmly uphold the principle of freedom of speech and expression as guaranteed under Article 19(1)(a) of the Constitution of India, and I respect the diverse viewpoints and expressions of all readers.

ppp

Other Books Of The Author

1. Empowering Minds: A Journey into Women's Self-Discovery and Power
2. The Dynamics of Motivation: Catalyzing Thought into Action
3. Meditation and Mental Well Being: The Path to Inner Peace and Clarity
4. The Psychology of Child Education: Nurturing Future Generations
5. Ethical Enlightenment: A Modern Guide to Living with Integrity
6. Voices of Empowerment: Stories of Women Rising Against Odds
7. Social Psychology in Everyday Life: Understanding Human Connections
8. The Essence of Motivational Speaking: Inspiring Change in Others
9. Balancing Acts: Women, Work, and the Will to Lead
10. Guiding with Grace: Raising Children with Compassion and Awareness
11. The Power of Positive Aging: Embracing Life After Fifty
12. Building Resilient Communities: Social Work in Action
13. The Ethical Educator: Principles for Teaching and Learning
14. From Insight to Impact: Social Psychology for a Better World
15. The Ethics of Empathy: A Guide to Ethical Living
16. The Science of Empowering the Self: Navigating Life's Challenges with Psychological Wisdom
17. The Mindful Conscious Leader: Meditation Techniques for Modern Management
18. Pioneering Spirit: Women's Pathways to Leadership and Empowerment
19. Feeling to Healing: The Role of Emotional Intelligence in Child Development
20. Transformative Talks and Words of Inspiration: Insights into Motivational Oratory

21. Green Ethics: A Path to Sustainable Living
22. Spiritual Integrity: Navigating Life with Moral Compassion
23. Clean Living, Clean Society: The Ethics of Cleanliness
24. Patriotic Spirits: Building a Nation on Positive Attitudes
25. Innovative Integrity & Vibrant Visions: The Ethical and Entrepreneurial Spirit of Gujarat
26. Youthful Visions, Endless Possibilities: Inspiring Ethics and Motivation in Children
27. Living Your Legacy: How to Motivate Others by Living Your Values
28. Secret of Healing Conversations: Ethical Practices in Counselling and Therapy
29. Creative Kindness: Crafting a Life of Compassion and Creativity
30. The Power of Appreciation: How Gratitude Can Transform Your Relationships
31. Bhagavad-Gita: Messages
32. Science of Art: The New Frontier of Fashion Modernism
33. Vivekananda's Virtues: A Blueprint for Modern Living
34. Empower Her: Navigating the Path to Women's Entrepreneurship
35. The Boundless Classroom: Innovations in Global Education
36. The Language of Leadership: Communicating with Authenticity and Impact
37. The Warrior's Mantra: Deciphering the Hanuman Chalisa
38. Echoes of Empathy: Transformative Stories of Social Service
39. Artful Living: Cultivating Creativity in Your Daily Routine
40. Finding Your Why: Discovering Your Passions and Charting Your Course
41. The Role of Social Media in Shaping Self-Esteem and Interpersonal Relationships among Adolescents
42. Karma's Tapestry: Weaving a Life of Selfless Service
43. Altruistic Alchemy: Transforming Lives Through Giving
44. The Blueprint of Pro-Activeness and Productivity: Crafting Habits for Success
45. The Simplicity with Grounded Wisdom: Embracing Authenticity

in a Complex World

46. Secret of Solopreneur's Odyssey: Navigating the Path to Self-Employment
47. Exploring Tapestry of Peace: Global Perspectives on Harmony
48. The Art and Actions of Connection: Mastering Communication for Impact
49. She Governs and at the Helm: Strategies for Political Empowerment
50. Rising Above and Rising with Grace: A Woman's Roadmap to Career Mastery
51. The Effect of Networking & Connectedness: Building Strategic Alliances for Women
52. Beyond his Barriers: Women Thriving in Male-Dominated Fields
53. Secret of Inner Compass: Navigating Life with Intuition
54. Creative & Pro-Active Muses: A Celebration of Women in the Arts
55. Unburdened: The Art of Releasing the Past
56. Amplified Voices: Speeches of Women that Astonished the World
57. Secret of Manifesting Dreams: A Woman's Guide to Intentional Living
58. Ethics and Value Based Education: Reimagining Japan's School System
59. The Moral Compass Curriculum: A Holistic Approach
60. Tech with Heart: Integrating Ethics into Digital Learning
61. Honoring Virtue: Recognizing Ethical Excellence in Education
62. Raising Good Humans: A Guide to Character Development
63. The Spark Within: Nurturing Creativity in Children
64. The Teenager Whisperer: Navigating Adolescence with Grace
65. Igniting a Passion for Learning: Inspiring Lifelong Curiosity
66. The Habit Lab: Cultivating Positive Behaviors in Children
67. Seeds of Empathy: Fostering Compassion in Young Hearts
68. The Reading Revolution: Inspiring a Love of Books in Children
69. The Learning Brain: Unlocking the Secrets of Student Success
70. Teaching for All: Differentiated Instruction Strategies
71. The Time Alchemist: Mastering Time Management for Peak Performance

72. The Resilience Factor: Transforming Setbacks into Stepping Stones
73. The Healing Touch of Nature: An Introduction to Naturopathy
74. Echoes of the Past: Healing Through Past Life Regression
75. The Spiritual Healer's Handbook: Exploring Energy Medicine
76. Crystal Clarity: Unveiling the Power of Gemstones
77. The Dream Weaver's Guide: Decoding the Language of Dreams
78. Emotional Alchemy: Transforming Pain into Power
79. Sonic Serenity: Harnessing Sound for Stress Relief
80. The Entrepreneur's Playbook: Launching Your Business with Confidence
81. Productivity Unleashed: Time Management Strategies for Entrepreneurs
82. The Problem Solver's Toolkit: Creative Solutions for Business Challenges
83. The Future is Now: Emerging Trends in Business
84. The Curious Explorer: A Child's Guide to Scientific Discovery
85. Digital Pioneers: Empowering Kids in the Tech World
86. The Young Philosopher's Guide: Exploring Life's Big Questions
87. Finding Your Voice: Communication Skills for Confident Kids
88. Nature's Playground: A Child's Guide to Outdoor Adventure
89. Growing a Greener Tomorrow: A Guide to Tree Planting & Conservation
90. Driving with Purpose: Ethical Choices on the Road
91. The Healing Touch: Cultivating Compassion in Healthcare
92. Navigating the Digital Landscape: Ethics in the Age of Social Media
93. The Ethical Closet: A Guide to Sustainable Fashion
94. The Mindful Voyager: Sustainable Travel Practices
95. The Feminine Divine: Honoring the Goddesses of India
96. Sacred Sounds: Chanting Your Way to Inner Peace
97. The Yoga Path: Uniting with the Divine Within
98. Rites of Passage: Creating Meaningful Ceremonies
99. The Chakra System: A Map of Inner Transformation
100. Spiritual Sangha: Finding Community through Satsang and

Bhajan

101. Pilgrimage of the Soul: Spiritual Journeys in India

ÞÞÞ

Contact

Dr. Minakshi Bansal
Social Activist
Ahmedabad, Gujarat, Bharat
minakshiindiag20@yahoo.com

❦❦❦

|| LOKAHA SAMASTHAHA SUKHINO BHAVANTU ||